WAGES OF INDEPENDENCE

Published in cooperation with the
Society for Historians of the
Early American Republic

EDITED BY PAUL A. GILJE

WAGES OF INDEPENDENCE

Capitalism in the Early American Republic

MADISON HOUSE

Madison 1997

Gilje, Paul A., EDITOR
Wages of Independence: Capitalism in the Early American Republic

Copyright © 1997 by Madison House Publishers, Inc. All rights reserved.

LIBRARY OF CONGRESS CATALOGING-IN-PUBLICATION DATA

Wages of independence : capitalism in the early American republic /edited by
    Paul A. Gilje.
        p. cm.
    Includes bibliographical references and index.
    Contents: The rise of capitalism in the early republic / Paul A. Gilje —
    The woman who wasn't there : women's market labor and the transition
    to capitalism in the United States / Jeanne Boydston — Markets without a
    market revolution : Southern planters and capitalism / Douglas R.
    Egerton — Rural America and the transition to capitalism / Christopher
    Clark — Capitalism, industrialization, and the factory in post-revolutionary
    America / Jonathan Prude — Artisans and capitalist development / Rich-
    ard Stott — Capitalizing hope : economic thought and the early national
    economy / Cathy D. Matson — The enemy is us : democratic capitalism in
    the early republic / Gordon S. Wood.
        ISBN 0-945612-53-2 — ISBN 0-945612-52-4 (pbk.)
        1. United States—Economic conditions—To 1865. 2. United States—
    Social conditions—To 1865. 3. United States—History—1815–1861. 4. Capi-
    talism—United States—History—19th century. 5. Finance—United States—
    History—19th century. 6. Transportation—United States—History—19th
    century. 7. Industrialization—United States—History—19th century. 8. United
    States—Commerce—History—19th century. I. Gilje, Paul A., 1951-   .
    HC105.W315   1997
    330.973—dc   97-2173
                                                                               CIP

Published in cooperation with the Society for Historians of
the Early American Republic.

Designed by Gregory M. Britton.

Printed in the United States of America on acid free paper.

Published by Madison House Publishers, Inc.
P. O. Box 3100, Madison, Wisconsin 53704

FIRST EDITION

CONTENTS

PREFACE

THE PURPOSE OF THIS SYMPOSIUM IS TO ALLOW the contributing scholars to summarize where we are in our examination of the rise of capitalism in the early republic, and to suggest where we might still go. Each author was asked to write in the specific area of his or her expertise, but all were given free rein to take their essays where they wanted to go. They were encouraged to mix primary and secondary sources as they pleased. The resulting eight essays cover a wide range of topics and allow us to see the lines of debate over the rise of capitalism.

The essay by Jeanne Boydston highlights the historical centrality of women and issues of gender. Boydston rightly argues that women were often at the core of the transformation to capitalism, and she demonstrates that the political trends of the day emphasizing independence were skewed to favor men and minimized the significance of women. In traditional society women played crucial roles in the local market place. Any changes in prices resulting from capitalist transformation were felt first by women. Boydston also reminds us that women's work often was diverse. Whether in the barnyard milking cows and making cheese, or in the house producing handiwork like brooms and straw hats, the flexible nature of women's work brought their labor most rapidly into the capitalist sphere. Women were among the first people to enter the factory as laborers. Yet, the role of women in the transformation to capitalism all too often has been missed because of the degradation of women and women's labor, not only by the males of the early nineteenth century but also by middle-class women who espoused the virtues of republican motherhood.

If women occupied a central role in the story of the rise of capitalism in America, what about other groups that were politically disfranchised? Douglas Egerton explores the relationship between slavery and capitalism. As Egerton points out, this relationship has been an area of intense debate among historians. Some scholars see slaveowners as would be entrepreneurs and slavery as an important component of capitalist development. Others, like Egerton, view slavery as more anomalous. While participating in a market for their export commodity, and while buying and selling labor, slaveholders and slavery remained, from this perspective, attached to a noncapitalist ethos in an economy dominated by unfree labor.

Others in southern society were even more isolated from the capitalist ethos. Egerton believes the upcountry yeoman clung to traditional non-capitalist economic ideas throughout the antebellum period. This position, as Christopher Clark points out stood in contrast to the situation of their northern agrarian cousins. Clark's essay emphasizes the regional nature of economic development. The question of slavery dominates the South, and Clark's views parallel Egerton's. Clark, however, stresses that while the situation may have varied from region to region, in New England, the mid-Atlantic, and in the West, free labor and the market economy allowed capitalism to flourish and ultimately contributed to industrial development.

Jonathan Prude's essay centers on that industrialization. He asks us to rethink the process of industrialization and the factory that has been its trademark. Prude expands the definition of factory beyond the hide-bound focus on big machinery and larger work force. He suggests that the key element of the factory was the breakdown of production into different parts to increase output and profits. So conceived, the new system worked its transformation not just in solid factories tucked along millstreams or dominated by smokestacks but in smaller workshops as well, where a variety of changes in the mode of production had a profound influence on American society, culture, and politics.

There are striking similarities between Prude's approach and Richard Stott's essay. Stott, too, stresses the significance of the division of labor rather than mechanization to economic change. He also challenges many of the common assumptions that have dominated labor history for the past twenty years. Stott calls into question the idea of artisan republicanism built upon a declension model. Instead, he urges us to look at artisans in both the cities and the countryside and to recognize that if some artisans slid down the economic scale in the first half of the nineteenth century, many others moved up. Stott even goes so far as to question the idealized vision many scholars have of the preindustrial work-shop. Stott calls for a more realistic version of the artisan's story, reflecting the full spectrum of experiences from the shoemaker who felt his world slipping away to the artisan would-be entrepre-neur seeking the main chance.

The artisan-on-the-make became one key element of a middle group that emerged as the centerpiece of the new economy envi-sioned by many nineteenth-century writers like Henry C. Carey. As Cathy Matson reminds us, the great economic change affecting the lives traced by these historians did not occur in a political and intellectual vacuum. Americans thought hard about what direc-tion their economy should take. Matson reviews for us the outlines of this debate as it took shape in the late eighteenth and early nineteenth centuries in four central areas: land, commerce, bank-ing, and manufacturing. The United States Constitution may have created a single national entity, but the role that new nation would fulfill in the emerging economy, and whether those developments were positive or negative, became areas of intense discussion.

Gordon Wood is also concerned with the middle group in society. He argues that the most important distinction in the early national period was not between capitalist and noncapitalist, but between those who labored and those who did not. The laborers were not driven by any class animus, and included among their number the poor and the affluent, as long as they were tied to-gether by their respect for work. In this survey of the debate over the economic transition of the early republic, Wood suggests that it was the Jeffersonians who most emphatically maintained the sanc-tity of work that fostered capitalism, and they form a conceptual bridge from that era to the present.

These essays do not cover all of the issues in the debate over the rise of capitalism after the American Revolution. They offer a broad range of interpretation that allows the reader to see where many of the main lines of argument lay. Some of the essays are more polemical than others, some concentrate on primary sources, others on the work of historians. Each adds to our understanding of a problem that is fundamental to the early republic and the molding of the American nation.

SEVERAL INDIVIDUALS PLAYED KEY ROLES IN making this volume possible. First, I thank John Larson and Mike Morrison for their help in putting together this symposium and guiding this volume into its book form. I also want to single out Maria Drake for all that she did during editing and the production of this book. John and Mike are blessed to have such a talented and efficient person working for them. Second, two key officers of the Society of Historians of the Early American Republic deserve recognition in ensuring that the society provided the financial backing for this volume. Jim Bradford had only just assumed the mantle of executive secretary, when he was confronted with an unprecedented request to publish this book. That he took this risk bodes well for the society under his direction. Peter Onuf, president of SHEAR, also threw his support behind this publication venture. His one time St. Louis amigo is grateful for his friendship and support.

The book would not have seen its way to publication without the aid of Gregory M. Britton, director of Madison House. He has moved this book along at a speed that boggles the mind and that will make the book available for classroom use within months of his agreement to publish.

Finally, the editor wants to thank the authors of the individual essays. The quality of scholarship and writing was so high, that there was little for him to do, other than to dot a few "i"s and cross a few "t"s. It has been a pleasure to work with each of the authors and to produce a collection that, it is hoped, will have some impact on the study of capitalism in the early republic.

PAUL A. GILJE
Norman, Oklahoma

O N E

The Rise of Capitalism in the Early Republic

PAUL A. GILJE

WHY IS THE STUDY OF THE RISE of capitalism important in the early republic? Twenty-five years ago most historians of the early republic assumed capitalism as a constant and focused largely on political issues; the controversies between Hamilton and Jefferson, the origins of the War of 1812, and the nature of Jacksonian democracy dominated their scholarship. Since that time some scholars have argued that capitalism was not always a part of the American mentality, and there has been an upsurge of new studies examining society and the economy as well as politics. Focusing on the rise of capitalism allows us to see the intersection of these three areas.[1]

The early republic, it turns out, was *a* crucial, if not *the* crucial, period in the development of that trademark characteristic of American society and economy, modern capitalism. In some degree Carl Degler was right to declare that capitalism came in the first ships bringing Europeans to the New World.[2] Fernand Braudel, too, was correct when he traced the emergence of western capitalism to the development of city states at the end of the medieval period.[3] But here we are interested not with the origins of capitalism but with its rise to a point where it permeated and affected a large component of American society. We are concerned with how capitalism crept into the consciousness of men and women, be they from merchant, farming, artisan, or laboring families.

Capitalism, however, is a slippery concept widely debated by historians. Some scholars search for the emergence of a capitalist system that controls the economy. Others are concerned with the dominance of certain structures and power relations where the capitalists not only own the means of production, but also hold the reins of political power. Some scholars center their analysis around the triumph of commercial transactions over many paternalistic social connections and sentimental attachments. Still others look for capitalistic behaviors and the adoption of core values rooted in individualism, competition, and the arbitration of market mechanisms.[4] No introductory essay will resolve this debate, and each contributor to the symposium that follows approaches the subject from his or her own unique perspective. Here I will briefly examine the salient areas of the transition to capitalism during the early republic and suggest what it is that concentrates these developments in this period.

In surveying the rise of capitalism in the early republic, we must be aware that in this period capitalism itself remained in its adolescence. Vibrant, cocky, feeling its own strength, and ready to take on the world, it was not the full-blown mature system of billion-dollar corporations, industrial development, urban sprawl, and intricate international financing that took shape by the end of the century. Yet as we stare into the exuberance of its youth, we can delineate many of the outlines of the capitalist system far more clearly than we could from its embryonic earlier expressions in the colonial and medieval periods. The capitalism locked in the holds of the *Santa Maria,* the *Susan Constant,* the *Mayflower,* and the *Arabella,* or confined within the walls of Pisa, Florence, Venice, and Genoa scarcely matched the system that forged the steel and oil empires of Andrew Carnegie and John D. Rockefeller. The early republic, in this longer view of history, emerges as a key transitionary period. More than that, it was in this period that many of the later elements of capitalism—a flexible currency, banking, corporations, transportation systems, industrialization, and pervasive consumerism—began to take on a recognizable shape.

The first of these characteristics concerns money. A capitalistic system must have a fluid, expansive, and extensive money supply. If it is somewhat inflationary, thus encouraging investment and borrowing, so much the better. During the early republic government and private enterprise combined to provide a dynamic currency. Both the Continental Congress and the individual state legislatures, based on colonial precedent, printed vast quantities of fiat currency to fund the War for Independence. Although these measures proved hyperinflationary in the short term, efforts undertaken by several states during the 1780s and by the national government under Hamilton's program in the 1790s, helped stabilize the monetary situation. The United States Constitution prevented states from printing their own money, and the federal government, although expanding a capital market in government bonds, also discontinued the practice of issuing paper currency.[5] Into this void stepped a new institution for the American economy—the bank.

Banks as institutions were marvelous (and I do not mean this term in a necessarily positive manner) tools for creating capital. They literally pulled money out of thin air. Before 1781 there were no banks in what was to become the United States. In 1781 Robert Morris organized the Bank of North America, followed by two other institutions in the 1780s and then by Hamilton's Bank of the United States in 1791. Thereafter banks began to proliferate as states issued charter after charter so that by the 1830s there were over two thousand banks spread across the United States. Each of these institutions printed its own notes, creating a patchwork currency that boggles the mind in terms of size, color, and design. Although this lack of consistency proved confusing (and a boon to counterfeiters) it worked wonders during the early republic by providing both a means of exchange, and increasing levels of capital for investment. These banks printed more currency than their net worth and cash reserves. This new money was then invested in land, mercantile activities, transportation facilities, even industrial production, fabricating more wealth which might be used to underwrite more banks, which printed more money, which expanded the economy further. Bank directors had no qualms about lending themselves money to underwrite their investment in the bank and in other forms of enterprise. Of course there were times when these inflationary bubbles would burst, but inevitably the cycle would start up again, driven, in part by the creative energies of bankers.[6]

Americans did not invent banking, they democratized it. Initially banks even in the United States were elitist institutions. Robert Morris intended his bank as an aid to public finance and as means to facilitate mercantile activity.[7] Likewise, Hamilton planned for the Bank of the United States to have a privileged relationship with the federal government. The United States owned one fifth of the bank, allowed the bank to hold its cash, and used the bank as its financial instrument. Hamilton intended to tie the monied interest to the national government through the Bank of the United States.[8] But privilege in the increasingly egalitarian United States was difficult to maintain. Other groups quickly petitioned for their own banks, and although it was a struggle at first, soon almost anyone with capital could form their own bank. Even the Bank of the United States, often attacked as monopolistic, spread its wealth by establishing quasi-independent branch banks. Banks, in other words, provided the capital that became the driving engine of the American economy. Insider trading, the loaning of money by the bank directors to themselves that would be decried today as illegal, fostered this democracy by allowing small shareholders and depositors to participate in the capital investments of the large shareholders.[9]

Another signal characteristic of the rise of American capitalism was the emergence of the corporation as a vehicle of capital investment. The reason why banks became democratized was that they relied on charters of incorporation from elected governments. Corporations originally were special grants of privilege (often a monopoly) to private individuals to pursue an activity for the general welfare. Morris, Hamilton, and the other men who organized the first banks argued that their institutions would pursue the public good. In the years that followed, that notion deteriorated, and a new understanding of "corporation" evolved. Privilege might have survived if it did not have to rely on elected officials from a broadening electorate of white adult males. Under a barrage of attacks about whose welfare was being furthered, all economic activity began to be seen as pursuing the public good and corporations became a means to pool investment resources for banks as well as many other enterprises. By the 1820s and 1830s the state legislatures became so inundated with petitions for incorporation that they passed laws of general incorporation that sidestepped the questioning of public good and opened this tool of capitalism to any would-be entrepreneur. At the same time the legal system moved to extend the concept of limited liability to all corporations. Although this provision was not completely in place until the 1850s, the courts before that decade protected the assets of most investors not dedicated to the specific corporation. Risk became encouraged, investments proliferated, and capitalism expanded.[10]

Banks were not the only type of enterprise to incorporate during this period. Crucial to the spread of capitalism was the development of rapid transportation which was often underwritten by state charters. Beginning with the turnpike boom of the 1790s and early 1800s, followed by the canal boom of the 1820s and 1830s, followed in turn by the railroad boom of the 1840s and 1850s, investors poured millions into internal improvements. So extensive were these investments, that notes issued by many of these companies joined the myriad of bank notes and passed as currency. More important was the impact that transportation facilities had on expanding the market economy. Previously fifty or sixty miles might prove too costly of a barrier for a farmer to overcome. But the building of a turnpike, canal, or railroad dramatically altered the situation: goods could travel scores, hundreds, even thousands of miles and still bring a profit. Shoes from New England found their way to the South. Meat from Ohio made it to the New York market. Grains no longer had to be converted to alcohol to cross the mountains.[11] An ambitious paper maker could travel to Berkshire County, Massachusetts, establish a mill, confident that he could obtain raw materials and specialty equipment and get his product to distant retailers.[12] News as well as products traveled across country, informing merchants where a likely investment should be made, or where their goods would find a ready market.[13]

Directly connected to the transportation revolution was another important aspect of the rise of capitalism in the early republic—expansion onto the frontier. What concerns us here is not just that a great migration occurred but how it was funded. While there were plenty of squatters who shifted from one frontier to another, the real story of the frontier in this period is more directly connected to the rise of capitalism. One of the great areas of speculation remained land. Fortunes were won and lost by men who managed to buy, connive, or swindle large tracts of land. The Revolutionary War, the establishment of the national domain, the federal land sale system, and the creation of new states provided ample opportunities for the would-be capitalist.[14] When William Cooper established Cooperstown in New York State he not only had to patent the land and plan its settlement, he also had to underwrite many who purchased his real estate by offering generous terms. Often he accepted a mortgage that merely promised payment in the future. The pioneer farmer, in turn, came to this bargain in the hope that his improvements and future gains would be enough to offset his debt.[15] As banks proliferated, they, too, were swept up in the expansion, funding loans for land and extending money for equipment on the will-o-the-wisp hope that the future would increase the value of every investment.[16]

Transportation also had a major impact on another element of the rise of American capitalism after the American Revolution: changes in the mode of production. Initially this change did not necessarily entail what has traditionally been called industrialization—the production of goods through the use of machines in factories. Artisans, for example, began to hire more half-skilled labor and took less care in training their apprentices as they broke down the process of production into different stages to increase output and to meet new market demands.[17] Likewise, some entrepreneurs relied increasingly on outwork, production outside the shop, which might use child or female labor as well as the handiwork of a journeyman. The beginning of the expansion of the shoe industry in Lynn, Massachusetts, followed this path. Only later, when costs could be decreased even further with machinery, did shoe production concentrate in factories.[18] Industrialization began in textiles as mills crowded the streams of New England and the mid-Atlantic states. By the 1820s and 1830s this industrialization relied increasingly on capital from banks and corporations.[19]

Crucial to the changed modes of production was the rise of consumerism. More and more Americans desired and could purchase goods. The source behind this consumerism is hard to delineate. Richard Bushman suggests that it came from a democratized sense of gentility that permeated many levels of society. As Americans strove toward respectability, so the argument goes, they desired more manufactured goods. This demand increased production, which increased overall wealth, which again increased demand, creating another cycle that fueled the fires of capitalism.[20] Regardless of its cause, as more Americans ate off plates instead of wood platters, sat on chairs instead of stools, sought the comfort and illumination of a lantern instead of candles or the fireplace at night, bought ready-to-wear clothes instead of donning homespun, and purchased any one of hundreds of items that they perceived would ease their lives, they not only altered their own daily world but contributed to a great transformation in the American economy.[21]

All of the elements briefly outlined above were intimately related. The final component of the rise of capitalism in the early republic is the most difficult to get a handle on; it is the mindset–mentality–of capitalism. Before independence many Americans clung to a set of values that emphasized family and the community. In the years after the Revolutionary War that began to change, especially in the North and Northeast. Capitalism started to reach into the workshop as well as the farmstead, creating acquisitive entrepreneurs. The capitalist mindset saw the production of more capital as its basic end and espoused values of hard work and delayed gratification that in the nineteenth century became identified as middle class. The rate and extent of this change varied greatly from individual to individual and group to group. One of the keys to understanding the early republic is to be found in the study of the impact of the rise of capitalism on individuals and groups. Recent studies have suggested that questions of gender, race, and ethnicity are as important as class and politics in our analysis of this period.[22] Not every American came to the capitalist point of view by 1848, and not every American holds this view today; but enough Americans started to examine the world from this perspective that we can talk with some authority about the rise of capitalism during the early republic.[23]

But why did capitalism develop so rapidly during the early republic? An answer to this question has been suggested already: the American Revolution and independence opened up new vistas that ultimately accelerated and reshaped developments already under way.

Capitalism did not simply emerge from a blank slate after 1776. Throughout the colonial period, and even long before, this economic system had been germinating, spreading, and transforming the western world. Money obviously underwrote market exchanges across the Atlantic. Colonists were innovative in the passage of fiat currency throughout the eighteenth century. Banks developed on the European continent and in England during the early modern period. Corporations were used to fuel overseas enterprise including many English efforts at colonizing North America in the guise of the Virginia Company, the Plymouth Company, and the Massachusetts Bay Company. Change in transportation technology is what brought Europeans out into the Atlantic world and facilitated their conquering overseas empires. The first American frontier for Europeans was the Atlantic coastline. Changes in the modes of production, affecting the supply of products and the demand for raw materials, began in England by 1750, and had already fueled a growing consumerism—an empire of goods in T. H. Breen's words— in the colonial world. And some colonial Americans had imbibed deeply of the capitalist ethic.[24]

In fact, in many ways the American Revolution began as a revolt against these tendencies. As every scholar knows, republican ideology of the American Revolution was a complex body of thought that included many different strands. Historians have debated vehemently over whether republicanism was based in classical thought emphasizing a virtue centered on the common good, or liberal ideas that released individuals to pursue their own interests. Over the last few years the debate appears to be resolving itself with compromise: republicanism entailed both.[25] I would take this last position one step further and suggest that these two strands of republicanism, and others less germane to the issue of capitalism, were mixed together within the minds of most Americans, swirling about, often leading to a babel of expressions that late twentieth-century historians have labored tortuously to delineate.

The classical side of republicanism's appeal was its critique of the spreading self-interested capitalism, best seen in the rampant consumerism of the mid-eighteenth century. Many Americans jumped on the bandwagon of resistance to imperial regulation because it was often cast in terms of denying both consumerism and capitalism. Nonimportation thus had a special attraction by declaring that Americans were too virtuous to need the imported luxury items. The wearing of homespun became a symbol of this resistance. Even members of the elite felt compelled to conform to this knew standard.[26] The fear, best expressed by Tom Paine in *Common Sense,* was that Americans had to revolt now, in 1776, before it was too late and they became corrupted like their fellow Englishmen.[27]

The irony of this position was that the effort to turn back the clock to a world that never was, merely moved the hands of the clock along at an ever-faster pace. If both classical and liberal strands of republicanism were inexorably intertwined in a Gordian Knot in 1776, the forces unleashed by the conflict for independence and the ensuing decades of adjustment, unraveled that tangled mesh as surely as did Alexander's sword, leaving the classical cord dangling, and the liberal cord as the main string of American ideology.[28]

The great pull of the liberal side of republicanism was that it released the individual to act for his own benefit and trumpeted the independent citizen. Conditions produced by the Revolutionary War combined with the creation of new governments and the expanding ideas about equality during the early republic to foster the spread of capitalism.

The immediate impact of the war was to create havoc. Armies marched across the landscape cutting swathes of devastation in their wake. But armies also had to eat. While sometimes they just took what they wanted, more often they bought supplies. Opportunities abounded for farmers to enter the market place and reap great profits.[29] One measure of the new prospects offered by the spread of this market economy is the amount of opposition to the consequent rise in prices. Market regulation became an issue that sharply divided Americans. Before the Revolutionary War there were less than a handful of market riots. During the conflict, scores of disturbances broke out in which crowds insisted on a just price for food.[30]

The war led to other economic problems. These difficulties may have hurt some while creating opportunities for others. Hyperinflation kicked in as the Continental Congress printed money to support the war. Anyone with a set income or who held the notes for too long was bound to loose. Inflationary economies help borrowers and allow individuals to make a financial killing when they quickly move property and goods back and forth for cash. Many people lost property during the war. But one person's loss often was another's gain. William Cooper managed to finagle his claim to the land around Lake Otsego because the Tory William Franklin was unable to protect his title in the New York State legal system.[31] Those who took risks—an important capitalist trait—might win or lose. Those who failed to do so, were likely to see their wherewithal decline.[32]

Beyond the war itself, independence liberated Americans from the British imperial system. While colonial status did not necessarily deter American economic development—the colonies sustained the highest economic growth in the eighteenth-century world—the end of the connection allowed the United States to move in new directions that encouraged the development of capitalism even more.[33]

The American government based its foreign policy on commerce and sought open markets. European powers resisted this trend, but the French Revolutionary and Napoleonic Wars compelled a partial backing down from this position, allowing American merchants to reap great profits as neutral carriers. Although eventually it became impossible for the United States to sustain its neutrality, with constant war scares, embargoes, and the War of 1812 disrupting trade, profits earned in this sector of the economy were plowed into other sectors. A war-ravaged Europe with huge armies to feed screamed for American foodstuffs, dragging more and more farmers into the market economy. Both before and after Waterloo the industrial revolution in England fostered exports of cotton that spurred both the southern and northern economies.[34]

Americans did not limit their trading to North Atlantic waters. They continued to send ships to the West Indies and sought new markets throughout the world. In 1784 the first American ship sailed for China. Soon a thriving Pacific trade developed bringing teas, dinnerware, and a wide assortment of items. The revolutions in Latin America spurred more enterprise. The hides that William Henry Dana describes as being collected in Mexican California fed the growing shoe industry of New England. Whalers plied all oceans, from frigid to torrid waters, searching for the oil that illuminated the homes of consuming Americans. American commerce and clipper ship technology soon became the envy of the world.[35]

The expansion of settlement by Euro-Americans that followed the American Revolutionary War was a disaster for Native Americans. Indians east of the Mississippi found themselves besieged by white Americans seeking to occupy their land. Unleashed from the limitations imposed during the colonial period by the alliance between the French and Indians and the Proclamation of 1763, white Americans poured into frontier regions of Maine, upstate New York, and across the Appalachians. Native Americans were trampled upon and moved out of the way. It is not as if Indians did not resist. The inexorable march of the frontiersman was not really inexorable; he often was halted and cast back. But the line of settlement from 1789 to 1848 moved from the Appalachians to beyond the Mississippi in a tremendous transformation that included wars of annihilation, Indian removal, and the re-settlement of millions of white and black Americans.[36] Again William Cooper stands as an example of how white Americans took advantage of this situation. Cooper could not have hoped to move farmers around Lake Otsego had the Iroquois, most of whom had sided with the British, still held the power that had enabled them to survive for two centuries nudged between the empires of competing European nations. Cooper, who strove to join an American political elite, as well as those already there like George Washington, planned to profit by land speculation.[37] Even the federal government, which benefited financially from settlement through its sale of public lands, got into the act. This combined onslaught sealed the fate of the Indians.[38]

As suggested in the example of Indian relations, the American Revolution led to the creation of government policies that fostered capitalist development through regulations and through law. Even under the Articles of Confederation the Northwest and Land Ordinances set a precedent for settlement, development, and incorporation of new territory within the United States.[39] After the Constitution created a stronger national government, the fiscal plan of Hamilton established a stable currency, secured confidence in government bonds, and provided an atmosphere conducive to capitalist development that was not reversed by the Jeffersonian Revolution of 1800.[40] As early as 1790, Congress passed a patent law to reward technological advances that could further economic growth.[41] Despite vacillations on bankruptcy law, Congress usually worked in support of investment.[42] The

Supreme Court moved even more forcefully to bolster capitalism, declaring the sanctity of the corporation in the *Dartmouth College* case (1819), while protecting innovation over prerogative in the *Charles River Bridge* decision (1836).[43]

These efforts were echoed on the state level. James Madison complained before the Constitutional Convention of the mutability of laws in state legislatures and the ability of economic interests to pass legislation on behalf of their own cause. The frame of government drawn up in the summer of 1787 may have reduced this multiplicity, however some flexibility in favor of these interest groups ultimately fostered capitalism. State governments issued the charters of incorporation that became the investment seedbeds of new enterprises.[44] States also poured resources into internal improvements. The Erie Canal became the example *par excellence* of how a state sponsored project could transform a region's economy and served as a model followed by many other states.[45] State courts, too, issued decision after decision concerning riparian rights, the nature of corporations, and land development that together furthered the cause of capitalism.[46]

Ultimately, the impact of the American Revolution on capitalism had its greatest effect on the individual. The American Revolution transformed the social landscape from a world that emphasized hierarchy and communal goals, to a world marked by equality and individualism—from classical to liberal republicanism.[47] This seismic shift did not occur overnight. Winifred Rothenburg argues that this change took place in rural Massachusetts shortly after 1785, with the increase in investment portfolios among middling farmers and the spread of consistent labor and farm prices.[48] Whether it occurred this early in Massachusetts or elsewhere is less important than the fact that it did occur during the early republic. There is no one date that we can point to that delineates one world from the other. Anachronisms remained in the nineteenth century as surely as there were precursors in the eighteenth century. But somewhere, somehow, something dramatic happened in the minds of many Americans; they began to seek gain through capitalist enterprise. For this reason, the rise of capitalism has become an area of major interest for the historians of this period.

NOTES

1. Three articles in the late 1970s served as the clarion for a reappraisal of the assumption that America was always capitalistic: Michael Merrill, "'Cash is Good to Eat': Self-Sufficiency and Exchange in the Rural Economy of the United States," *Radical History Review*, 4 (Winter 1977), 42–71; Robert E. Mutch, "Yeoman and merchant in pre-Industrial America: eighteenth-century Massachusetts as a case study," *Societas*, 7 (Autumn 1977), 279–302; and James A. Henretta, "Families and Farms: *Mentalité* in Pre-Industrial America," *William and Mary Quarterly*, 35 (Jan. 1978), 3–32.

2. Carl Degler, *Out of Our Past: The Forces that Shaped Modern America* (1959; 3d. ed., New York, 1984), 1–8. For an interesting discussion of the capitalism on those ships, see Marcus Rediker, *Between the Devil and the Deep Blue Sea: Merchant Seamen, Pirates, and the Anglo-American Maritime World, 1700–1750* (Cambridge, 1987).

3. Fernand Braudel, *Civilization and Capitalism, 15th–18th Century*, Vol. I: *The Structures of Everyday Life*, trans. Sian Reynolds (3 vols., New York, 1981–1984), 479–558; Braudel, *Civilization and Capitalism*, II, 232–49; Braudel, *Capitalism and Material Life, 1400–1800*, trans. Miriam Kochan (New York, 1973), 373–440.

4. For good summaries of the debate, see Allan Kulikoff, "The Transition to Capitalism in Rural America," *William and Mary Quarterly*, 46 (Jan. 1989), 120–44; Michael Merrill, "Putting 'Capitalism' in Its Place: A Review of Recent Literature," *ibid.*, 52 (April 1995), 315–26; Christopher Clark, "Economics and Culture: Opening Up the Rural History of the Early American Northeast," *American Quarterly*, 43 (June 1991), 279–301; Paul E. Johnson, "The Market Revolution" in Mary Kupiec Cayton *et al.*, eds., *Encyclopedia of American Social History* (3 vols., New York, 1993), I, 545–60; Jack Larkin, "Massachusetts Enters the Marketplace, 1790–1860," in Martin Kaufman *et al.*, eds. *A Guide to the History of Massachusetts* (New York, 1988), 69–82; Robert E. Mutch, "Colonial America and the Debate About Transition to Capitalism," *Theory and Society*, 9 (Nov. 1980), 847–63; Winifred Barr Rothenberg, "The Bound Prometheus," *Reviews in American History*, 15 (Dec. 1987), 628–37; Daniel Vickers, "The Transition to Capitalism in the American Northeast," *History Teacher*, 27 (May 1994), 267–69; and Thomas S. Wermuth, "Were Early Americans Capitalists? An Overview of the Development of Capitalist Values and Beliefs in Early America, *Mid-America*, 74 (Jan. 1992), 85–97. For major statements in the debate, see Jeremy Atack and Fred Bateman, *To Their Own Soil: Agriculture in the Antebellum North* (Ames, 1987); Atack and Bateman, "Yeoman Farming: Antebellum America's Other 'Peculiar Institution,'" in Lou Ferleger, ed., *Agriculture and National Development: Views on the Nineteenth*

Century (Ames, 1990), 25–51; Hal S. Barron, *Those Who Stayed Behind: Rural Society in Nineteenth-Century New England* (Cambridge, 1984); Michael A. Bernstein and Sean Wilentz, "Marketing, Commerce, and Capitalism in Rural Massachusetts," *Journal of Economic History,* 44 (March 1984), 171–73; John L. Brooke, *The Heart of the Commonwealth: Society and Political Culture in Worcester County, Massachusetts, 1713–1861* (Cambridge, 1989); Richard L. Bushman, "Family Security in the Transition from Farm to City, 1750–1850," *Journal of Family History,* 6 (July 1981), 238–56; Christopher Clark, *The Roots of Rural Capitalism: Western Massachusetts, 1780–1860* (Ithaca, 1990); Steven Hahn and Jonathan Prude, eds., *The Countryside in the Age of Capitalist Transformation: Essays in the Social History of Rural America* (Chapel Hill, 1985); James A. Henretta, *The Origins of American Capitalism: Collected Essays* (Boston, 1991); Stephen Innes, *Creating the Commonwealth: The Economic Culture of Puritan New England* (New York, 1995); Innes, ed., *Work and Labor in Early America* (Chapel Hill, 1988); Allan Kulikoff, *The Agrarian Origins of American Capitalism* (Charlottesville, 1992); James T. Lemon, *The Best Poor Man's Country: A Geographical Study of Early Southeastern Pennsylvania* (Baltimore, 1972); Michael Merrill, "The Anticapitalist Origins of the United States," *Review: Fernand Braudel Center,* 13 (Fall 1990), 465–97; Merrill, "'Capitalism' and Capitalism," *History Teacher,* 27 (May 1994), 277–80; Merrill and Sean Wilentz, eds., *The Key of Liberty: The Life and Democratic Writings of William Manning, "A Laborer," 1747–1814* (Cambridge, MA, 1993); Gregory H. Nobles, "The Rise of Merchants in Rural Market Towns: A Case Study of Eighteenth-Century Northampton, Massachusetts," *Journal of Social History,* 24 (Fall 1990), 5–23; Nancy Grey Osterud, "Gender and the Transition to Capitalism in Rural America," *Agricultural History,* 67 (Spring 1993), 14–29; Osterud, "Gender and the Capitalist Transition in Rural America," *History Teacher,* 27 (May 1994), 273–76; Bettye Hobbs Pruitt, "Self-Sufficiency and the Agricultural Economy," *William and Mary Quarterly,* 41 (July 1984), 333–64; Marcus Rediker, "'Good Hands, Stout Heart, and Fast Feet': The History and Culture of Working People in Early America," *Labour,* 10 (Autumn 1982), 123–44; Winifred Barr Rothenberg, "The Market and Massachusetts Farmers, 1750–1855," *Journal of Economic History,* 41 (June 1981), 283–314; Rothenberg, "The Market and Massachusetts Farmers: Reply," *ibid.,* 43 (June 1983), 479–80; Rothenberg, "Markets, Values and Capitalism: A Discourse on Method," *ibid.,* 44 (March 1984), 174–78; Rothenberg, "The Emergence of a Capital Market in Rural Massachusetts, 1730–1838," *ibid.,* 45 (Dec. 1985), 781–808; Rothenberg, "The Emergence of Farm Labor Markets and the Transformation of the Rural Economy: Massachusetts, 1750–1855," *ibid.,* 48 (Sept. 1988), 537–66; Rothenberg, *From Market Places to a Market Economy: The Transformation of Rural Massachusetts, 1750–*

1850 (Chicago, 1992); Carole Shammas, "Consumer Behavior in Colonial America," *Social Science History*, 6 (Winter 1982), 67–86; Daniel Vickers, "Competency and Competition: Economic Culture in Early America," *William and Mary Quarterly*, 47 (Jan. 1990), 3–29; Vickers, *Farmers and Fishermen: Two Centuries of Work in Essex County, Massachusetts, 1630–1850* (Chapel Hill, 1994); Rona S. Weiss, "The Market and Massachusetts Farmers, 1750–1850: Comment," *Journal of Economic History*, 43 (June 1983), 475–78; and Stephanie Grauman Wolf, *Urban Village: Population, Community, and Family Structure in Germantown, Pennsylvania, 1683–1800* (Princeton, 1976). For a synthetic discussion of the period, see Gordon S. Wood, *The Radicalism of the American Revolution* (New York, 1991); and Charles G. Sellers, *The Market Revolution, 1815–1846* (New York, 1991). See also Sean Wilentz, "Society, Politics, and the Market Revolution, 1815–1848," in Eric Foner, ed., *The New American History* (Philadelphia, 1990), 51–71.

5. E. James Ferguson, *The Power of the Purse: A History of American Public Finance, 1776–1790* (Chapel Hill, 1961); Ferguson, "Political Economy, Public Liberty, and the Formation of the Constitution," *William and Mary Quarterly*, 40 (July 1983), 389–412; Drew R. McCoy, *The Elusive Republic: Political Economy in Jeffersonian America* (Chapel Hill, 1980); Janet A. Riesman, "Money, Credit, and Federalist Political Economy," in Richard Beeman, Stephen Botein, and Edward C. Carter II, eds., *Beyond Confederation: Origins of the Constitution and American National Identity* (Chapel Hill, 1987), 128–61; Edwin J. Perkins, *American Public Finance and Financial Services, 1700–1815* (Columbus, OH, 1994); Gerald Stourzh, *Alexander Hamilton and the Idea of Republican Government* (Stanford, 1970).

6. Naomi R. Lamoreaux, *Insider Lending: Banks, Personal Connections, and Economic Development in Industrial New England* (Cambridge, 1994). The definitive work on banking remains Bray Hammond, *Banks and Politics in America, From the Revolution to the Civil War* (Princeton, 1957). See also Robert M. Blackson, "Pennsylvania Banks and the Panic of 1819: A Reinterpretation," *Journal of the Early Republic*, 9 (Fall 1989), 335–58.

7. Thomas M. Doerflinger, *A Vigorous Spirit of Enterprise: Merchants and Economic Development in Revolutionary Philadelphia* (Chapel Hill, 1986), 268–73, 296–310; Hammond, *Banks and Politics*, 40–64.

8. McCoy, *Elusive Republic*, 147–52.

9. Hammond, *Banks and Politics*, 144–71, 572–630; Lamoreaux, *Insider Lending*.

10. Robert F. Dalzell, Jr., *Enterprising Elite: The Boston Associates and the World They Made* (Cambridge, MA, 1987); L. Ray Gunn, *The Decline of Authority: Public Economic Policy and Political Development in New York, 1800–1860* (Ithaca, 1988); Hendrik Hartog, *Public Property and Private Power:*

The Corporation of the City of New York in American Law, 1730–1870 (Chapel Hill, 1983); Oscar Handlin and Mary Flug Handlin, *Commonwealth: A Study of the Role of Government in the American Economy: Massachusetts, 1774–1861*, (1947; 2d. ed., Cambridge, MA, 1969); William E. Nelson, *Americanization of the Common Law: The Impact of Legal Change on Massachusetts Society, 1760–1830* (Cambridge, MA, 1975), 133–36.

11. The pathbreaking work remains George Rogers Taylor, *The Transportation Revolution, 1815–1856* (New York, 1951). See also John Lauritz Larson, "'Bind the Republic Together': The National Union and the Struggle for a System of Internal Improvements," *Journal of American History*, 74 (Sept. 1987), 363–87; Larson, "A Bridge, a Dam, a River: Liberty and Innovation in the Early Republic," *Journal of the Early Republic*, 7 (Winter 1987), 351–75; and Ronald E. Shaw, *Canals for a Nation: The Canal Era in the United States, 1790–1860* (Lexington, 1990).

12. Judith A. McGaw, *Most Wonderful Machine: Mechanization and Social Change in Berkshire Paper Making, 1801–1885* (Princeton, 1987), 15–37.

13. Richard D. Brown, *Knowledge is Power: The Diffusion of Information in Early America, 1700–1865* (New York, 1989); Richard R. John, *Spreading the News: The American Postal System from Franklin to Morse* (Cambridge, MA, 1995); Taylor, *Transportation Revolution*, 132–52.

14. Stephen Aron, "The Significance of the Frontier in the Transition to Capitalism," *History Teacher*, 27 (May 1994), 270–72; Allan G. Bogue, *From Prairie to Corn Belt: Farming on the Illinois and Iowa Prairies in the Nineteenth Century* (Chicago, 1963), 169–81; Jacob E. Cooke, *Tench Coxe and the Early Republic* (Chapel Hill, 1978), 79–82, 311–33; Don Harrison Doyle, *The Social Order of a Frontier Community: Jacksonville, Illinois, 1825–1870* (Urbana, 1978); David Maldwyn Ellis, *Landlords and Farmers in the Hudson-Mohawk Region, 1790–1850* (Ithaca, 1946); John Mack Faragher, *Sugar Creek: Life on the Illinois Prairie* (New Haven, 1986); Daniel Feller, *The Public Lands in Jacksonian Politics* (Madison, 1984); Susan E. Gray, "Local Speculator as Confidence Man: Mumford Eldred, Jr., and the Michigan Land Rush," *Journal of the Early Republic*, 10 (Fall 1990), 383–406; William H. Siles, "Pioneering in the Genesee Country: Entrepreneurial Strategy and the Concept of a Central Place," in Manfred Jonas and Robert V. Wells, eds., *New Opportunities in a New Nation: The Development of New York After the Revolution* (Schenectady, 1982), 35–68; Alan Taylor, *Liberty Men and Great Proprietors: The Revolutionary Settlement on the Maine Frontier, 1760–1820* (Chapel Hill, 1990); Richard C. Wade, *The Urban Frontier: Pioneer Life in Early Pittsburgh, Cincinnati, Lexington, Louisville, and St. Louis* (Chicago, 1959).

15. Alan Taylor, *William Cooper's Town: Power and Persuasion on the Frontier of the Early American Republic* (New York, 1995), 86–138.

16. Hammond, *Banks and Politics*, 279–85, 622–30.

17. John R. Commons, "American Shoemakers, 1648–1895: A Sketch of Industrial Evolution," *Quarterly Journal of Economics*, 24 (Nov. 1909), 39–84; Christine Daniels, "'WANTED: A Blacksmith Who Understands Plantation Work': Artisans in Maryland, 1700–1800," *William and Mary Quarterly*, 50 (Oct. 1993), 743–67; Eric Foner, *Tom Paine and Revolutionary America* (New York, 1976); Susan E. Hirsch, *Roots of the American Working Class: The Industrialization of Crafts in Newark, 1800–1860* (Philadelphia, 1978); Paul E. Johnson, *A Shopkeeper's Millennium: Society and Revivals in Rochester, New York, 1815–1837* (New York, 1978); Gary J. Kornblith, "The Artisanal Response to Capitalist Transformation," *Journal of the Early Republic*, 10 (Fall 1990), 315–21; Kornblith, "'Cementing the Mechanic Interest': Origins of the Providence Association of Mechanics and Manufacturers," *ibid.*, 8 (Winter 1988), 355–87; Bruce Laurie, *Artisans into Workers: Labor in Nineteenth-Century America* (New York, 1989); Laurie, *Working People of Philadelphia, 1800–1850* (Philadelphia. 1980); Staughton Lynd, "The Mechanics in New York Politics, 1774–1788," *Labor History*, 5 (Fall 1964), 225–46; David Montgomery, "The Working Classes of the Pre-Industrial American City, 1780–1830" *Labor History*, 9 (Winter 1968), 3–22; Gary B. Nash, *The Urban Crucible: Social Change, Political Consciousness, and the Origins of the American Revolution* (Cambridge, MA, 1979); Charles S. Olton, *Artisans for Independence: Philadelphia Mechanics and the American Revolution* (Syracuse, 1975); Howard B. Rock, *Artisans of the New Republic: The Tradesmen of New York City in the Age of Jefferson* (New York, 1979); Rock, Paul A. Gilje, and Robert Asher, eds. *American Artisans: Crafting Social Identity, 1750–1850* (Baltimore, 1995); W. J. Rorabaugh, *The Craft Apprentice: From Franklin to the Machine Age in America* (New York, 1986); Steven J. Ross, *Workers On the Edge: Work, Leisure, and Politics in Industrializing Cincinnati, 1788–1890* (New York, 1985); Sharon V. Salinger, *"To Serve Well and Faithfully:" Labor and Indentured Servants in Pennsylvania, 1682–1800* (New York, 1987); Ronald Schultz, *The Republic of Labor: Philadelphia Artisans and the Politics of Class, 1720–1830* (New York, 1993); Billy G. Smith, *The "Lower Sort:" Philadelphia's Laboring People, 1750–1800* (Ithaca, 1990); Charles G. Steffen, *The Mechanics of Baltimore: Workers and Politics in the Age of Revolution, 1763–1812* (Urbana, 1984); Richard B. Stott, *Workers in the Metropolis: Class, Ethnicity, and Youth in Antebellum New York City* (Ithaca, 1990); Sean Wilentz, *Chants Democratic: New York City & the Rise of the American Working Class, 1788–1850* (New York, 1984); Wilentz, "Against Exceptionalism: Class Consciousness and the American Labor Movement, 1790–1920," *International Labor and Working Class History*, 26 (Fall, 1984), 1–24; Alfred F. Young, "The Mechanics and the Jeffersonians: New York, 1789–1801," *Labor History*, 5 (Fall 1964), 247–76.

18. Alan Dawley, *Class and Community: The Industrial Revolution in Lynn* (Cambridge. MA, 1976); Paul G. Faler, *Mechanics and Manufacturers in the Early Industrial Revolution: Lynn, Massachusetts, 1780–1860* (Albany, 1981).

19. Mary H. Blewett, *Men, Women, and Work: Class, Gender, and Protest in the New England Shoe Industry, 1780–1910* (Urbana, 1988); Thomas C. Cochran, *Frontiers of Change: Early Industrialism in America* (New York, 1981); Dalzell, *Enterprising Elite*; Thomas Dublin, *Women at Work: The Transformation of Work and Community in Lowell, Massachusetts, 1826–1860* (New York, 1979); Teresa Anne Murphy, *Ten Hours' Labor: Religion, Reform, and Gender in Early New England* (Ithaca, 1992); Paul F. Paskoff, *Industrial Evolution: Organization, Structure, and Growth of the Pennsylvania Iron Industry, 1750–1860* (Baltimore, 1983); Jonathan Prude, *The Coming of Industrial Order: Town and Factory Life in Rural Massachusetts, 1810–1860* (Cambridge, 1983); Philip Scranton, *Proprietary Capitalism: The Textile Manufacture at Philadelphia, 1800–1885* (Cambridge, 1983); Cynthia J. Shelton, *The Mills of Manayunk: Industrialization and Social Conflict in the Philadelphia Region, 1787–1837* (Baltimore, 1986); Barbara M. Tucker, *Samuel Slater and the Origins of the American Textile Industry, 1790–1860* (Ithaca, 1984); Anthony F. C. Wallace, *Rockdale: The Growth of an American Village in the Early Industrial Revolution* (New York, 1978); Norman Ware, *The Industrial Worker, 1840–1860: The Reaction of American Industrial Society to the Advance of the Industrial Revolution* (1924; rep., Chicago, 1964); David A. Zonderman, *Aspirations and Anxieties: New England Workers and the Mechanized Factory System, 1815–1850* (New York, 1992).

20. Richard L. Bushman, *The Refinement of America: Persons, Houses, Cities* (New York, 1992).

21. Cary Carson, Ronald Hoffman, and Peter J. Albert, eds., *Of Consuming Interests: The Style of Life in the Eighteenth Century* (Charlottesville, 1994); James Deetz, *In Small Things Forgotten: The Archaeology of Early American Life* (New York, 1977); Elisabeth Donaghy Garrett, *"At Home": The American Family, 1750–1850* (Garden City, NY, 1990); David Jaffee, "Peddlers of Progress and the Transformation of the Rural North, 1760–1850," *Journal of American History*, 78 (Sept. 1991), 511–35; Jack Larkin, *The Reshaping of Everyday Life, 1790–1840* (New York, 1988); Neil McKendrick, John Brewer, and J. H. Plumb, *The Birth of a Consumer Society: The Commercialization of Eighteenth-Century England* (Bloomington, 1982); Sally McMurry, *Families and Farmhouses in Nineteenth-Century America: Vernacular Design and Social Change* (New York, 1988); Jane C. Nylander, *Our Own Snug Fireside: Images of the New England Home, 1760–1860* (New York, 1993); Elizabeth A. Perkins, "The Consumer Frontier: Household Consumption in Early Kentucky," *Journal of American History*, 78 (Sept. 1991), 486–510.

22. The best discussions of gender are Jeanne Boydston, *Home and Work: Housework, Wages, and the Ideology of Labor in the Early Republic* (New York, 1990); Dublin, *Women at Work*; Joan M. Jensen, *Loosening the Bonds: Mid-Atlantic Farm Women, 1750–1850* (New Haven, 1986); Suzanne Lebsock, *The Free Women of Petersburg: Status and Culture in a Southern Town, 1784–1860* (New York, 1984); and Christine Stansell, *City of Women: Sex and Class in New York, 1789–1860* (New York, 1986). For race, see John W. Blassingame, *The Slave Community: Plantation Life in the Antebellum South*, (1972; 3d. ed., New York, 1979); Eugene D. Genovese, *Roll, Jordan Role: The World the Slaves Made* (1974; 2d. ed., New York, 1976); Philip D. Morgan, "Work and Culture: The Task System and the World of Lowcountry Blacks, 1700 to 1880," *William and Mary Quarterly*, 39 (Oct. 1982), 563–99. For a recent discussion of the role of ethnicity, see Stott, *Workers in the Metropolis*; and Peter Way, *Common Labour: Workers and the Digging of North American Canals, 1780–1860* (Cambridge, 1993).

23. For the English background, see Alan Macfarlane, *The Origins of English Individualism: The Family, Property and Social Transition* (New York, 1978); Macfarlane, *The Culture of Capitalism* (New York, 1987). For developments in the United States, see Stuart M. Blumin, *The Emergence of the Middle Class: Social Experience in the American City, 1760–1900* (Cambridge, 1989); Doerflinger, *A Vigorous Spirit of Enterprise*; Jonathan A. Glickstein, *Concepts of Free Labor in Antebellum America* (New Haven, 1991); David Jaffee, "The Village Enlightenment in New England, 1760–1820," *William and Mary Quarterly*, 47 (July 1990), 327–46; Gary J. Kornblith and John M. Murrin, "The Making and Unmaking of an American Ruling Class," in Alfred F. Young, ed., *Beyond the American Revolution: Explorations in the History of American Radicalism* (Dekalb, 1993), 27–79; Mary P. Ryan, *Cradle of the Middle Class: The Family in Oneida County, New York, 1790–1865* (Cambridge, 1981); Steven Watts, *The Republic Reborn: War and the Making of Liberal America, 1790–1820* (Baltimore, 1987); and Wood, *Radicalism of the American Revolution*, 347–69.

24. T. H. Breen, "An Empire of Goods: The Anglicization of Colonial America, 1690–1776," *Journal of British Studies*, 25 (Oct. 1986), 467–99; Breen, "Narrative of Commercial Life: Consumption, Ideology, and Community on the Eve of the American Revolution," *William and Mary Quarterly*, 50 (July 1993), 471–501; J. E. Crowley, *This Sheba, Self: The Conceptualization of Economic Life in Eighteenth-Century America* (Baltimore, 1974); Innes, *Creating the Commonwealth*; Carole Shammas, *The Pre-industrial Consumer in England and America* (New York, 1990).

25. For efforts at synthesis, see Joyce Appleby, *Liberalism and Republicanism in the Historical Imagination* (Cambridge, MA, 1992); Linda K. Kerber, "The Republican Ideology of the Revolutionary Generation," *American Quarterly*, 37 (Fall 1985), 474–95; Milton M. Klein, Richard D.

Brown, and John B. Hench, eds., *The Republican Synthesis Revisited: Essays in Honor of George Athan Billias* (Worcester, 1992); James T. Kloppenberg, "The Political Virtues of Liberalism: Christianity, Republicanism, and Ethics in Early American Discourse," *Journal of American History*, 74 (June 1987), 9–33; Isaac Kramnick, "The 'Great National Discussion': The Discourse of Politics in 1787," *William and Mary Quarterly*, 45 (Jan. 1988), 3–32; and Robert E. Shalhope, *The Roots of Democracy: American Thought and Culture, 1760–1800* (Boston, 1990). For articulation of the classical side of the debate, see Shalhope, "Toward a Republican Synthesis: The Emergence of an Understanding of Republicanism in American Historiography," *William and Mary Quarterly*, 29 (Jan. 1972), 49–80; and Shalhope, "Republicanism and Early American Historiography," *ibid.*, 39 (April 1982), 334–56. For articulation of the liberal side of the debate, see Joyce Appleby, "Republicanism and Ideology," *American Quarterly*, 37 (Fall 1985), 461–73; and Appleby, *Capitalism and a New Social Order: The Republican Vision of the 1790s* (New York, 1984).

26. Gordon S. Wood, *The Creation of the American Republic, 1776–1787* (Chapel Hill, 1969), 91–124; and Paul A. Gilje, *The Road to Mobocracy: Popular Disorder in New York City, 1763–1834*, (Chapel Hill, 1987), 44–52.

27. Thomas Paine, *Common Sense*, ed. Isaac Kramnick (London, 1976), 81–96.

28. Wood, *Radicalism of the American Revolution*.

29. Edward Countryman, "The Uses of Capital in Revolutionary America: The Case of the New York Loyalist Merchants," *William and Mary Quarterly*, 49 (Jan. 1992), 3–28; Countryman, "'To Secure the Blessings of Liberty': Language, the Revolution, and American Capitalism," in Young. ed., *Beyond the American Revolution*, 123–48; James A. Henretta, "The War for Independence and American Economic Development," in Henretta, *Origins of American Capitalism*, 203–55.

30. Barbara Clark Smith, "Food Rioters and the American Revolution," *William and Mary Quarterly*, 51 (Jan. 1994), 3–33.

31. Taylor, *William Cooper's Town*, 65–70.

32. Doerflinger, *A Vigorous Spirit of Enterprise*, 197–250; Ferguson, *Power of the Purse*, 3–105.

33. Alice Hanson Jones, *Wealth of a Nation to Be: The American Colonies on the Eve of the Revolution* (New York, 1980); John J. McCusker and Russell R. Menard, *The Economy of British America, 1607–1789* (Chapel Hill, 1985); Edwin J. Perkins, *The Economy of Colonial America*, (1980; 2d. ed., New York, 1988).

34. Anna Cornelia Clauder, *American Commerce as Affected By the Wars of the French Revolution and Napoleon, 1793–1812* (Philadelphia, 1932); John E. Crowley, *The Privileges of Independence: Neomercantilism and the Ameri-*

can Revolution (Baltimore, 1993); Felix Gilbert, *To the Farewell Address: Ideas of Early American Foreign Policy* (Princeton, 1961); McCoy, *Elusive Republic*; Cathy D. Matson and Peter S. Onuf, *A Union of Interests: Political and Economic Thought in Revolutionary America* (Lawrence, 1990); John R. Nelson, Jr., *Liberty and Property: Political Economy and Policymaking in the New Nation, 1789–1812* (Baltimore, 1987); Douglass C. North, *The Economic Growth of the United States, 1790–1860* (New York, 1961).

35. Richard Henry Dana, Jr., *Two Years Before the Mast*, ed. Thomas Philbrick (New York, 1981); Howard I. Chapelle, *The Search for Speed Under Sail, 1700–1855* (New York, 1967); Carl C. Cutler, *Greyhounds of the Sea: The Story of the American Clipper Ship*, (1930; 3d. ed., Annapolis, 1984); William H. Goetzmann, *New Lands, New Men: America and the Second Great Age of Discovery* (New York, 1986); Samuel Eliot Morison, *The Maritime History of Massachusetts, 1783–1860* (1923; 4th ed., Boston, 1979); Ralph D. Paine, *The Old Merchant Marine: A Chronicle of American Ships and Sailors* (New Haven, 1919).

36. Andrew R. L. Cayton and Peter S. Onuf, *The Midwest and the Nation: Rethinking the History of an American Region* (Bloomington, 1990); Allan Kulikoff, "Uprooted Peoples: Black Migrants in the Age of the American Revolution, 1790–1820," in Ira Berlin, and Ronald Hoffman, eds., *Slavery and Freedom in the Age of the American Revolution* (Charlottesville, 1983), 143–71; Alan Taylor, "Land and Liberty on the Post-Revolutionary Frontier," in David Thomas Konig, ed., *Devising Liberty: Preserving and Creating Freedom in the New American Republic* (Stanford, 1995), 81–108; Anthony F. C. Wallace, *The Long Bitter Trail: Andrew Jackson and the Indians* (New York, 1993); Richard White, *The Middle Ground: Indians, Empires, and Republics in the Great Lakes Region, 1650–1815* (Cambridge, 1991).

37. Taylor, *William Cooper's Town*, 34–40.

38. Aron, "The Significance of the Frontier," 270–72; Cayton and Onuf, *The Midwest and the Nation*; Feller, *Public Lands*; Malcolm J. Rohrbough, *The Trans-Appalachian Frontier: People, Societies, and Institutions, 1775–1850* (New York, 1978).

39. Peter S. Onuf, *Statehood and Union: A History of the Northwest Ordinance* (Bloomington, 1987).

40. McCoy, *Elusive Republic*, 185–235; Cooke, *Tench Coxe*, 155–523; James L. Huston, "The American Revolutionaries, the Political Economy of Aristocracy, and the American Concept of the Distribution of Wealth, 1765–1900," *American Historical Review*, 98 (Oct. 1993), 1079–1105.

41. Doron Ben-Atar, "Alexander Hamilton's Alternative: Technology Piracy and the Report on Manufactures," *William and Mary Quarterly*, 52 (July 1995), 389–414; Brook Hindle, *Emulation and Invention* (New York, 1981).

42. McCoy, *Elusive Republic*, 178–184.

43. Tony A. Freyer, "Negotiable Instruments and the Federal Courts in Antebellum American Business," *Business History Review*, 50 (Winter 1976), 435–55; Freyer, *Producers Versus Capitalists: Constitutional Conflict in Antebellum America* (Charlottesville, 1994); Stanley I. Kutler, *Privilege and Creative Destruction: The Charles River Bridge Case* (Philadelphia, 1971).

44. Gunn, *Decline of Authority*; Handlin and Handlin, *Commonwealth*, 87–202.

45. Robert Greenhalgh Albion, *The Rise of New York Port, 1815–1860* (1939; rep., Hamden, CT, 1961); Russell Bourne, *Floating West: The Erie and Other American Canals* (New York, 1992); Madeline Sadler Waggoner, *The Long Haul West: The Great Canal Era, 1817–1850* (New York, 1958); Taylor, *Transportation Revolution*, 15–131.

46. Handlin and Handlin, *Commonwealth*, 134–60; Morton J. Horwitz, *The Transformation of American Law, 1780–1860* (Cambridge, MA, 1977); Nelson, *Americanization of the Common Law*, 67–174; Freyer, *Producers Versus Capitalists*.

47. Wood, *Radicalism of the American Revolution.*.

48. Rothenberg, *From Market-Places to a Market Economy*, 113–47.

TWO

The Woman Who Wasn't There: Women's Market Labor and the Transition to Capitalism in the United States

JEANNE BOYDSTON

FEMALE WAGE-EARNERS OCCUPY an anomalous position in the story of the transition to capitalism in the United States. On the one hand, historians have documented the presence of large numbers of women in paid labor by the 1830s, specifically in key sectors of the new northeastern industrial labor force: textiles, shoe-making, and the early garment industry.[1] On the other hand, women and their paid work are virtually absent from narratives of the late eighteenth-century economic transformations that preceded and laid the foundations for early industrialization. That transition—from "market-places" to a "market economy," as Winifred Barr Rothenberg has framed it[2]—is represented as a story of the labor and economic decisions of men: male farmers reorienting their crops, male field workers entering into new labor contracts, male merchants venturing into new relations of credit and debt, and male artisans struggling against the demise of the craft shop. Only relatively late in the process, with the coming of the mills themselves, do women's market activities figure in any important way in accounts of the transition to capitalism.[3]

The absence of women and of women's market relations from this story reflects the ways in which we have approached both the history of women in the eighteenth century and the history of the market transition. Although the field of American women's history began with the question of the transition to capitalism, studies of the late eighteenth century (influenced by Mary Beth Norton's and Linda Kerber's fine early work on "Republican motherhood") remain preoccupied with prescription and ideology.[4] This accent has been encouraged by the last decade's consuming interest in "republicanism" and by the current postmodern turn away from social history. Recent research has focused on women's efforts to enter and shape the new "public" sphere—a project that tends to center studies of gender in intellectual history rather than in the history of material life and one that seldom encounters women in their daily market relations.[5]

Questions of the timing and nature of the transition to capitalism have thus become the province of economic and labor historians and historians of the working class.[6] As Allan Kulikoff has pointed out, this effort has not been particularly unified. While economic historians track the forces of the market, labor and working-class historians track the force of ordinary lives.[7] What the two groups have in common, however, in addition to a rough agreement on the timing (1750–1820) and unevenness of the transition, is a marked indifference to women, particularly to women's market activities. Perhaps because women's market labor was only rarely self-owned, labor historians presume it to have existed outside of, and been largely ineffectual in, the transition to a free labor economy.[8]

It is this virtual exclusion of women's market work from narratives of the transition that I wish to reexamine in the following pages. Read both through and, in a sense, against one another, recent work in women's history and in labor and economic history suggest that the material conditions of the transition may have given rise, not to the exclusion of women from the market, but to an expanded dependence on the market labor of women, performed both within and outside the household. In both its material and its ideological character, women's labor tended to be more flexible than the labor men performed—more easily adapted and redeployed to meet the changing needs of household economies. If anything, the transition moved many women into a more critical relation to the market. Ironically, this very aggressive presence of women in the transitional economy fostered their disappearance from its subsequent narratives.

There are several good reasons to undertake a reexamination of women's market labor in the transition, apart from simply improving our understanding of eighteenth-century women's history. American labor history remains a story dominated by men and told within a framework that does not easily accommodate the experiences of most women's lives. However many women in however many paid occupations are added to the canon, in American labor history, the "worker" remains resistently gendered male. Arguably, our understanding of the period of the transition provides a conceptual template for our understanding of subsequent labor history in America. Rethinking the processes through which America moved to a market economy may provide the analytical basis for reconceptualizing the larger history of paid labor.[9]

The revised narrative I propose focuses on the evolution of the market in the mid-Atlantic and northern states. But in its main outline and implications, the analysis is not exclusive to the North. Studies of North American slavery suggest related changes in the labor of enslaved African-American women in the late eighteenth century in response to developments of local, regional, and trans-Atlantic markets. More broadly, recent studies of the history of "race" in the early republic have begun to lay bare the very deep levels at which American notions of liberty and property for some were authorized in systems of dependency and unfreedom for others. Some of the most important of this work has focused on the discursive construction of the "free" market, arguing that the individualism of liberal economics was founded in the structural and ideological exclusion of certain categories of citizens from claims to market activity.[10]

Elsewhere I have argued that women's claim to property in their unpaid labor vanished in the construction of the wage labor market. As Thomas Dublin has accurately pointed out, however, industrialization "transformed . . . much of women's work into wage labor," making the story of women and the transition also the story of "the changing character of women's wage work."[11] That transformation commenced, I believe, not in the nineteenth century, but in the eighteenth.

A new narrative must begin in the households of late British colonial America, for it was as members of such households that most women—most non-Native people—initially experienced the transition to capitalism. The first eddies of that change teased their way into daily life erratically—a shortage of land for planting, a retailer pressing for more shoes to sell, a storekeeper willing to give credit for yarn, more notes in circulation, soldiers needing food, blankets, and shelter. Gradually, as transatlantic and local commerce increased in the first half of the eighteenth century, older relations of exchange began almost imperceptibly to weaken. The growth of commerce was first stalled and then severely interrupted by the political protests of mid-century: nonimportation agreements, trade disruption, shortages, eventually the war itself. Blockades and occupation played havoc with local economies. Peace brought little immediate relief: Great Britain did not reopen its empire to American trade; under the excuse of searching for renegade seamen, British ships preyed on American carriers; and British traders dumped goods on the American market at prices that undercut local production. As states levied new taxes to pay war debts and creditors pressed for compensation, paper money depreciated wildly. Some Americans did well, but, as Jean Lee has observed, for many Americans the founding years of the republic were comparable to the Great Depression of the 1930s. In this milieu, households struggled merely to stay afloat and maintain some semblance of control over their own economic lives.[12]

Although some people may have sought to avoid the increasing interdependencies of the economy, most free Americans lived in middling households that already were deeply, deliberately, and contentedly immersed in commercial relations. For them, the goal was not splendid isolation, but successful negotiation of the market, culminating, most people hoped, in only moderate social change and modest personal prosperity. In the phrase so often invoked in the late eighteenth century, free Americans sought a "competency"—a balancing of such strategies of both household and market production as might ensure economic security and perhaps a luxury or two. As Daniel Vickers has noted, Americans worried less about the abstract "legitimacy" of commercial relations than they did about protecting a competency within those relations.[13]

As had been the case in Europe, Americans' first and fail-safe strategies were domestic: members sought to secure and to increase household productivity—both for internal consumption and for the market. Although specific schemes for coping with the erratic economy varied from place to place, family to family, the range of personal adaptations by men to this new emphasis on household productivity has been documented fairly well: farming fathers geared their crops toward local urban demand, began to travel farther to market, added a cash-earning trade to their farming, opened a saw- or a grist-mill, contracted with "cottagers" to supply their labor needs, became involved in land speculation; and sons delayed marriage, abandoned farming for craft work, moved to the edges of white settlement in search of land.[14]

Generally less extensive than men's, women's paid labor and production for the market nonetheless also became important components of household economies by the middle of the eighteenth century. As recent work in women's history has demonstrated, this labor, too, provided an important resource for household adaptation during the transition to a market economy. Joan Jensen, who once observed that "the ideology of self-sufficiency of the New England farms in 1800 was based to a great extent on the ability of women in the household to provide a surplus for the local market," has shown that women's increased dairy production provided a source of capital for expanding family farming operations in the late eighteenth-century mid-Atlantic region. In the Chesapeake, women's spinning and weaving—"entirely absent in the mid-seventeenth century," according to Lois Green Carr and Lorena S. Walsh—had become consequential household industries by the mid-eighteenth century, providing cash and exchange commodities that ballasted the volatile market for tobacco. Faye E. Dudden has demonstrated the growing importance of a wide range of women's cash- or credit-producing work on late eighteenth- and early nineteenth-century northern farms, emphasizing that this labor was so profitable to household economies that mistresses would *spend* money hiring workers in order to *make* money selling the goods produced. Some rural women took jobs in small, local manufactories: for example, a pottery in East Caln Township in southeast-

ern Pennsylvania employed nine adults, five of them women. Females were among the children who went to work in the first Slater
mills. Other women—both wives and older daughters living at
home—earned wages in other peoples' homes by cooking, caring
for children, spinning flax and wool, milking and churning. Thomas Dublin has documented the steady and crucial spread of outwork—"[h]andloom weaving, shoe binding, the braiding of straw
and palmleaf hats, and sewing"—performed largely by women and
children, as a household economic strategy in New England from
1810 onward. It may well have been the general recognition that
rural households needed to hustle to stay afloat that encouraged
Alexander Hamilton and Tench Coxe to assume that farm women
and children (and old men) would be pleased to take in outwork
from early manufactories.[15]

Because the market transition threatened the customary bases
of manhood, women (and children) may disproportionately have
borne the brunt of the new pressures on household economies.
Revolutionary-era republicanism regarded male wage-earners with
skepticism—as dependants with uncertain claims to the full privileges of manhood. In her fine study of masculinity and eighteenth-
century commercial practices, Toby Ditz has argued that the "volu-
minous correspondence" of Philadelphia merchants on the
conditions of trade in the late 1790s amounts to "a sustained medi-
tation on the precariousness of male identity and reputation, a
precariousness linked not only to the competitiveness and volatility of markets but also to the difficulties of defining a reputable
self within the world of patronage and connection that still structured market relations."[16] Striving to represent themselves as persons of self-mastery, honest intent, and effectuality, the merchants
depicted their dependencies upon others as not dependencies at
all (dependence and patronage alike being highly suspect in the
new republican culture) but rather as forms of instrumentality.
Reliance upon the goodwill or financial investment of someone
else was thus transfigured from subordination into economic agency
and political virtue. In the chaotic world of revolutionary America,
men's claim to citizenship rested on forging this association of
maleness with economic agency, for it was in economic independence that political existence was understood to reside. Daniel
Vickers has similarly suggested that farming fathers were willing

to integrate outwork shoemaking into their household economies because it could be delegated to sons (and daughters), thus permitting the household head to distance himself from the taint of wage dependence.

But if eighteenth-century constructions of manhood proved problemmatic in the face of the market transition, female labor carried with it into the transition a long cultural assumption of flexibility in the form of the role of "deputy husband." Under the rubric of household necessity and with the approbation of the household head, a free female could engage in virtually any form of labor without censure. Women's customary labors may also have had a certain spatial and structural malleability lacked by men's: "women's work" often consisted of a greater variety of occupations than "men's work" and was performed within a comparatively smaller physical area (the homelot), where the tools necessary for shifting back and forth from one task to another could be readily at hand. The adjustments and improvisations required to negotiate the market may have been particularly compatible with this pattern of work.[17]

These changes may have had a more vivid impact on the social landscape of women's work in the cities than in the countryside. Although some rural woman surely increased their time working cash crops in the field, the more general rural pattern of intensifying women's labor in *household* production did not entail dramatically altered patterns of spatial mobility. Not so in the cities of the eastern seaboard. War-time occupation of the cities sent floods of refugees—and refugee households—into the countryside. The return of peace and rural dislocation echoed swells of population back into the cities. In this reconstituted urban landscape, women were everywhere visible as aggressive and ostensibly independent economic agents. They worked as sailors, morticians, day laborers, iron mongers, and money lenders, as well as seamstresses, mantuamakers, and milliners.[18] They claimed their place in the market assertively. When speculations on the debt of the new republic resulted in a financial panic in 1792, widows, market women, and prostitutes were included in the mobs of creditors threatening to "disembowel" the men they held responsible.[19]

Working women may have offered an unusually assertive urban presence in several other, related ways. Most of the early republic's working women were married, but a surprisingly large portion of urban households may have been female-headed. In the years after the war, many urban females were widows. They were joined by single female migrants from the countryside, seeking adventure, jobs, or both in the city. These women appear to have created occupational residential clusters, often choosing to live next-door to, or near, other female-headed laboring class households. In addition, migrants (men and women) may have been responsible for an unusually high post-war fertility rate, especially out of wedlock. Billy Smith has suggested that there was a "loosening of constraints on marriage" among new arrivals in Philadelphia. Finally, a visible minority of laboring urban women were African American, many of them newly freed in the wave of postrevolutionary emancipations. In fact, most women in postrevolutionary cities lived in male-headed households. But, as Billy Smith has pointed out, most non-elite households required the direct economic participation of both partners, often in ways that sent wives into the streets alongside female heads-of-household. All of these characteristics gave working women—whether they actually lived in male-headed households or not—an aggressive and ostensibly autonomous presence in the cities of the early republic.[20]

Ready enough to discover friction in other arenas of life during the transition to capitalism, historians have been loath to recognize that these internal household adjustments—present in the countryside, although more visible in the cities—could have created conflict between husbands and wives. As Allan Kulikoff declared in a discussion of the overlap of men's and women's responsibilities, "the presumption of household unity precludes the possibility of conflict or tension within households, especially between husbands and wives, over authority, the sexual division of labor, and the distribution of goods produced by members for consumption, exchange or sale."[21] To presume unity of this sort, however, is to presume more than the evidence will sustain. The point is not that marriages had suddenly become a battleground of individualistic interests, but that household relations had become markedly more complicated.

Carole Shammas's study of Bucks County, Pennsylvania, suggests other divergences of interest between husbands and wives.

Late seventeenth- and early eighteenth-century husbands tended to use their wills to protect their widows against the potential claims of sons, by providing more than a one-third share of the estate and by specifying the terms of the widow's maintenance. By the late eighteenth century, that practice had reversed. Husbands who left wills in the early republic tended to leave their wives less than the amount provided in intestacy laws and less than they had in earlier periods. As Shammas has observed, by the 1790s, "the presence of an adult son or sons shrank a widow's portion more severely than earlier, while wealth and the occupation of farming were somewhat less important." The presence of daughters had some effect in siphoning off the widow's portion (the more daughters the greater the impact) but less than the presence of any sons. Combined with the changes in the intestate laws, daughters were on the whole inheriting larger portions than earlier, but even those portions generally went into household pools under the legal direction of their husbands.[22] So long as principles of *feme covert* remained stubbornly embedded in the law, the growing importance of contract and free labor in the postrevolutionary United States could only put most women at a severe disadvantage.

On the other hand, their importance in household economies may well have encouraged in women a sense of competence and, in some degree, of social autonomy. The market transition gave new context to women's labor, within which the work gradually assumed new economic meanings and gave rise to new economic relations. We see this development clearly in women's dairying: the growth of markets for dairy products infused women's longstanding work in the barnyard (previously but one of many elements in farm well-being) with new economic importance and, potentially, new social power. The same transformation probably occurred in women's participation in family urban businesses and in the various forms of labor that were absorbed into the vast outwork networks of the early nineteenth century.

The same transformation probably lay behind women's participation in food riots during the revolutionary crisis. Barbara Clark Smith has noted that, in revolutionary America as in other preindustrial economies, women's customary economic responsibilities within the household included a certain right to bargain over prices, quarrel with vendors, even join mobs when the balance of community sentiment opposed specific merchant practices. By the mid 1770s, women were participating actively in food riots and antihoarding mobs that enforced non-consumption agreements and administered a "fair market" in the colonies. Smith has argued that women "conducted nearly one-third of the riots." Her evidence indicates that they participated in and or publicly supported many others.[23] Although Smith finds precedents for this female activism in earlier eighteenth-century events, women's participation in the food riots of the 1770s may have reflected their increased economic importance within their households—a heightened sense of the precariousness of their household economies and a greater readiness to take matters into their own hands. Smith's evidence would seem to suggest that women became more visible in these demonstrations as the war wore on.

Although much of the work on eighteenth-century women's history has focused on "Republican motherhood"—a slant that tends to emphasize the association of women with families—there is good reason to suspect that many women experienced the postrevolutionary years as a period of comparative practical self-reliance. Both Linda Kerber's and Mary Beth Norton's studies of women in the American Revolution indicate an increasing instrumentality over time. Certainly Laurel Thatcher Ulrich's *A Midwife's Tale* presents a story about a woman's practical daily autonomy and geographic mobility.[24] This view of women in the early republic is supported by Lisa Wilson Waciega's examination of widows in southeastern Pennsylvania, many of whom proved to be better entrepreneurs than their husbands, and by Susan Branson's work on Elizabeth Meredith, who could barely repress her self-satisfaction when she wrote proudly to her son in 1796, "your mother . . . though she is old and weak . . . still acquits herself with some degree of reputation, especially in the financing business."[25]

This fine sense of expansiveness—not yet diminished by the language of domesticity—may have motivated women's growing engagement in civic culture in the early republic, including the question of their own participation in the new government. Certainly, Abigail Adams, Mercy Otis Warren, Judith Sargent Murray, and the other women who argued for women's education and for an enlarged political role for women were influenced by European models like Catherine Macaulay and Mary Wollstonecraft. But they may also have been giving expression to a current of American female assertiveness. This is not to claim that the late eighteenth-century was a golden age for women, or that all women experienced the early republic in the same way. It is to suggest that the political crisis and economic transition contained possibilities for an enlarged sense of effectuality—that same sense of purpose and means that informed women's movement into voluntary reform in the early republic.[26]

It is unclear whether this pride was newly acquired during the Revolution, as Kerber and Norton suggest, or was, as I suspect, an expression of a practical daily self-assurance long familiar to women but since obscured in historians' preoccupation with ideology. What does seem apparent is that the economic transition and the political Revolution accentuated the daily plasticity of gender in colonial America, sometimes drawing men and women into social practices long implied but seldom enacted, sometimes seeming to yield wholly new meanings in the context of daily life. In the circumstances of the Revolution, for example, a food riot was potentially an act not merely of *moral* economy but of *political* economy. The point was not lost on Abigail Adams. In a letter to her husband, Adams described the mobbing of a merchant rumored to be hoarding coffee, observing that the riot was led by "A Number of females some say a hundred." "It was reported he had a Spanking among them," she remarked with studied insouciance, "but this I believe was not true." And then she added, anticipating what she undoubtedly assumed would be her husband's own reaction: "A large concourse of Men stood amazd silent Spectators of the whole transaction."[27]

The anecdote was a fable of the growing discomfort felt by many Americans at the sight of women's participation in such activities. Necessity had given rise to a healthy culture of "out-of-doors" politics[28] that, continuing past the rebellion, struck many elite Americans as at odds with the rational discourse required by republican government. Even if customary, the appearance of women in spontaneous and highly assertive contexts of political economy was particularly alarming. Vague although it remained, the political culture of the new nation clearly depended upon the proposition that public virtue and political voice rightly belonged to men, on the assumption that men, as creators and owners of wealth and property, would have sufficient stake in the new republic to act as its guides. Since women formerly had been viewed as important producers (although *not* owners) of wealth, the political revolution of the European enlightenment required that the status of producer be dissociated from women and exclusively associated with men. That the material conditions of the transition enlarged women's productive importance within their households heightened the urgency of that dissociation.

Although an increased household dependence on female labor has been identified as an element in the transition to capitalism in a number of European contexts, the cultural stakes may have been particularly high in America. Compared to Europeans, a far greater proportion of free Americans, both rural and urban, lived in relatively stable, independent, middling households at the time of the transition. That is to say, free Americans experienced the transition through the medium of relatively small and stable households, rather than as individuals, as members of communities of uprooted wage-laborers, or (to a lesser degree) as members of extended families. Furthermore, in America the transition to capitalism coincided with a political revolution that emphasized the bourgeois family and male economic independence. The two were linked in experience and compressed in time in a way that was far less the case in European countries.

This linkage—the material dependence on female labor within households joined to the growing ideological association of independent manhood with economic agency—may account for the peculiarly intense and sentimental character of American domesticity. The local, daily, personal conflicts created by economic change may not have seemed avoidable, but neither were they tolerable on a long-term basis. Thinking of the inter-household competition provoked by multiple families struggling to hold their own and yet depending on each other, Daniel Vickers has argued that one form of reconciliation came through the intensification of "domestic ritual" (episodes of neighborliness such as barn-raisings and church gatherings) that functioned to "mitigate ill-feeling and resolve disagreements . . . by bringing people into formal settings where they could reopen lines of communication that had stretched or even snapped in the course of working life."[29] The intense expressions of nuclear family feeling that came to characterize nineteenth-century American culture (and the enormous nostalgia with which nineteenth-century Americans would look back upon the revolutionary years) may have served parallel ends, reconciling an increased reliance upon female labor with a more formal male assertion of economic privilege through a romance of family culture.

As I have suggested elsewhere, the reverse also obtained: the market and market relations had begun to assume a distinctly masculine discursive character. There was, in particular, a new association of masculinity with trade and commerce—an assumption that "masculinity" was a condition that inhered in the prosecution of economic activity and the achieving of economic independence. To make this observation is not to argue that males had never earlier cared about economic power or employed economic yardsticks as a "measure of the man." Mary Beth Norton has noted the frequency with which men in seventeenth-century Maryland framed their criticisms of each other in terms of flawed business practice, while women were most likely to be defamed as whores or witches.[30]

In the years of the transition to capitalism, however, economic success became, not merely an important attribute but indeed one of the central constituting tropes of masculinity. Unsurprisingly, the most dramatic enactments of this exclusive gender claim to economic agency appear to have come from working men, who found their own labor at the center of a thoroughgoing reorganization and found themselves lacking the most public emblem of the new masculinity other than economic agency, the vote. Certainly, laboring men urged their own political vision—artisan republicanism—with an emphasis on maleness that utterly obliterated the presence of women in commerce and the trades. The famous Philadelphia "Federal procession" of July 4, 1788, held in celebration of the founding of the new republic, included axemen, dragoons, artillery, foreign consuls, architects, house-carpenters, the Agricultural Society, the Manufacturing Society, sail makers, ship carpenters, ship joiners, rope makers, merchants, traders, cordwainers, coach painters, cabinet makers, chair makers, brick makers, painters, draymen, clock and watchmakers, tailors, brickmakers, blacksmiths, hatters, potters, tallow chandlers, lawyers, physicians, clergy, and others. Some of these were occupations in which women participated, and yet in the entire procession there was evidently not a single female.[31]

Such an all-male parade was an enactment, in the concrete terms of craft insignia, of a far larger exclusion of women from the "public" sphere of the new nation, an exclusion expressed in commerce, politics, and civic debate, all of which spheres were constituted as gendered male. In its most formal manifestation, that exclusion was inscribed in the new federal Constitution, which fixed in law long-standing prejudices against females in office and denied to women direct participation in federal legislative debates over the direction of the republic's political economy.[32]

Women were also represented as incapable of entering the world of letters so central to the emergent bourgeois public sphere. Journalist William Cobbett lampooned both newspaper publisher Margaret Bache and author Susanna Rowson for their educational deficiencies: Bache's grammar and Rowson's use of figurative language. "I beg leave to observe," he wrote of Rowson in his broadside, *A Kick for a Bite*, "that, though tropes and figures are very useful things, when they fall into skillful hands, they are very dangerous, when they fall into those of a contrary description. When I see you flourishing with a metaphor, I feel as much anxiety as I do, when I see a child playing with a razor."[33] The metaphor associated language—the vehicle of public presentation—with the razor, a male instrument. It identified femaleness with childishness, a lack of skill, and a certain heedlessness, and stressed the dangers to females who played with the tools of public presence.

In an old libel now revisited with gusto, this supposed incapacity for participation in public debate was inscribed in the female body. Obviously, women continued to go about their daily business in their communities. But the female body asserted as an active public presence was rendered as a sign of social disorder. The only public commerce easily imaginable for a female was the commerce of her body. In *The Excellency of the Female Character Vindicated*, for example, Thomas Branagan complained that "We may even see the consorts and daughters of the guardians of the public weal strutting through the streets, with the disgraceful and obscene appearances peculiar to lewd women," and concluded that "the fashionable female, who exposes publicly what prudence should conceal, not only entices the male of ardent passions to perpetuate, but also commits the crime of sentimental fornication herself. . . ." "Prostitution" was the name given to female agency in the public realm.[34]

In contrast, the new republican female *ideal* expressed a certain public hesitation and incapacity—better yet, public absence. When depicted within households, women were romanticized as "Republican mothers" and cultivated companions—a nostalgic re-interpretation, I would suggest, of the increased dependence on their productive labors. Out-of-doors alternatives—that is to say, ways of expressing ideal womanhood out in the community, visible, active, and capable on the streets—became increasingly inaccessible in republican culture. By the beginning of the nineteenth century, the alternatives available to women who risked an active public presence would be figured in the correlatives of seduction and prostitution, the one implying public incapacity, the other flagrant public genius in a woman.[35]

The maleness constructed in this discourse appeared sometimes in manifestations of violent activity: Ditz's merchants, for example, imaged masculinity in furious storms, crashing thunder, damaging winds. But masculine agency in the early republic was most fundamentally enacted, not in violence, but in sheer presence. Indeed, the most important element of masculinity was the presentation of a simple, transparently capable self. Ditz notes the preoccupation of eighteenth-century merchants with themes of deceit and with "distinguish[ing] honorable from dishonorable conduct and men. . . ." The honorable man was the man who could present himself openly, disguising nothing, holding nothing back, available for inspection and scrutiny—the man fully exposed. In this rendering, as John Barrell has noted, passionate activity of any sort was unattractive in men, since strong drives, frantic motion, erratic conduct, could only smudge the highly prized image of "public plainness."[36]

The growing discursive animosity toward visible, laboring, ostensibly independent women did not come from men only. The history of women workers in the transition to capitalism is also preeminently a history of the changing practice of gender between and among women—a point made a quarter of a century ago by Gerda Lerner.[37] The response of elite women to the political and economic turmoil of the late eighteenth century was to separate themselves emotionally and rhetorically from working women.

For prosperous women, the process of withdrawing from bonds of familiarity (not equality, which had not existed) with working women was part of a process of moving toward an identification with the new social order, and particularly with the civic culture of the men of their class. After the Revolution a number of elite women (and some men) began to argue for the inclusion of women in the public culture through education. Men were likely to emphasize the advantages to husbands of educated partners: "To give us happiness, and to enable us to support the vicissitudes and misfortunes of the world, was the intention of a benevolent Deity, in adding women to the society of men," as John Swanwick explained in 1787 to the students of the Young Ladies' Academy in Philadelphia.[38] Elite women had mixed motives for advocating improved female education, among them the search for vehicles that would provide them greater instrumentality in the new republican civic culture.[39] But their arguments very often shared with men the assumption that women's activities should remain private, unrevealed, out of the observing eye. Susanna Rowson represented respectable womanhood as a retreat from publicity, counseling American women in her *Mentoria; or The Young Lady's Friend*: "True happiness . . . flies the glare of fashion, and the midnight revel. . . ."[40] The point was not that women were not smart, performed no function in the household economy, or had no thoughts to contribute to the new polity. The point was that women should exercise these functions undisclosed. It was in that lack of disclosure that "womanhood" existed.

This newly identified threat to the status of men in the republic, combined with the influences of European bourgeois culture, thus prompted elaborate new iterations on and revisions of older notions of colonial "vertuous housewifery," coming eventually to constitute that elaborate female domesticity that historians have identified with the antebellum era. By the early nineteenth century, female "domesticity" had assumed a particularly commercial stamp—or, rather, a particular anticommercial—stamp. Femaleness was inappropriate to the public realm of commerce and trade and could exist there only as a personal degradation (seduction) and a public danger (prostitution), both of these being monstrous abnormalities. While full public disclosure might be the mark of the honorable man, for women public visibility was the sign of dishonor and pollution. Female domesticity was thus constituted historically in the United States not simply as a discourse about males and females but as a discourse particularly about working women. In this idiom, the world of labor was, by definition, a male world and females who appeared in that world were engaging in unnatural relations. The growing ideological prohibition of female exposure soon assumed a particular association with women workers, as this group became the very embodiment of natural disorder. Republican political economy was figured in the aggressive presence of men and the emphatic absence of women.[41]

Prescription is seldom an adequate sole guide to daily experience—least so in times of rapid and profound change, when the search for order, becoming peculiarly urgent, is likely to produce highly stylized and unusually polarized representations of social life, almost by definition at odds with more local social practice. In such times, as Sean Wilentz has demonstrated in *Chants Democratic,* idealized identities are apt to be urged with particular (and particularly misleading) firmness: "artisan republicanism" prospered in New York City just as the artisan system began to give way to the bastard shop.

In the United States, the emergence of the ideology of separate spheres must be viewed at least in part as a hardening of the attitudes of certain groups against specific actual practices of gender they deemed particularly threatening during the political and economic revolutions. That is to say, although the tropes of separate spheres had begun to appear in the colonies by the early eighteenth century, representations of the protected household and the private female became conventionalized after the Revolution in part as a response to the exceptional volatility and permeability of households during the revolutionary era and to the changing practices of gender within households and throughout society more generally.

The refiguring of gender in the closing decades of the eighteenth century helped construct a culture in which "working woman" became a logical inconsistency—an oxymoron. This process was well underway by the time the female operatives entered the first Lowell mills, helping to construct their presence in the industrial labor force from the beginning as exceptional. The workplace was by definition male—not because only or mainly men inhabited it (they did not) but because femaleness had been defined successfully as absence from the work place. Of course women remained in the labor force, but always on the terms of outsiders having to make anew the case for their seriousness, their respectability, and their economic contribution.

NOTES

1. See, for example, Thomas Dublin, *Women at Work: The Transformation of Work and Community in Lowell, Massachusetts, 1826–1860* (New York, 1979); Joan M. Jensen, "Cloth, Butter and Boarders: Women's Household Production for the Market," *The Review of Radical Political Economy*, 12 (Summer 1980), 14–24; Jensen, "Butter Making and Economic Development in Mid-Atlantic America from 1750 to 1850," *Signs*, 13 (Summer 1988), 813–29; Jensen, *Loosening the Bonds: Mid-Atlantic Farm Women, 1750–1850* (New Haven, 1986); Alice Kessler-Harris, *Out to Work: A History of Wage-Earning Women in the United States* (New York, 1982); Christine Stansell, *City of Women: Sex and Class in New York, 1789–1860* (New York, 1986); Mary H. Blewett, *Men, Women, and Work: Class, Gender, and Protest in the New England Shoe Industry, 1780–1910* (Urbana, 1988); and Thomas Dublin, *Transforming Women's Work: New England Lives in the Industrial Revolution* (Ithaca, 1994).

2. Winifred Barr Rothenberg, *From Market-Places to a Market Economy: The Transformation of Rural Massachusetts, 1750–1850* (Chicago, 1992).

3. Women are of course treated in studies of the Lowell mills; see Dublin, *Women at Work*. With the exception of Mary Blewett's work, however, they have not been treated extensively in studies of New England shoemaking in the transition; see Blewett, *Men, Women, and Work*. They are almost entirely absent from general works on the transition. For full citations on the literature of the transition to capitalism, see note 4 in Paul A. Gilje, "The Rise of Capitalism," in this volume. Although women appear in economic history during the early years of the factory system, they disappear again once the factory system was established, and men had made their peace with wage labor, males poured into the jobs previously held by women. Having acted their brief hour upon the economic stage, female wage-earners then were heard no more for half a century.

4. See, for example, Linda K. Kerber, *Women of the Republic: Intellect and Ideology in Revolutionary America* (Chapel Hill, 1980); and Mary Beth Norton, *Liberty's Daughters: The Revolutionary Experience of American Women, 1750–1800* (Boston, 1980). For a critique of the paradigm of "re-

publican motherhood," see Margaret A. Nash, "Rethinking Republican Motherhood: Benjamin Rush and the Young Ladies' Academy of Philadelphia," *Journal of the Early Republic* (forthcoming). The field of United States women's history originated in questions about the transition to capitalism. Indeed, so prominently did the transition to capitalism figure in the first decade of work that women's historians were soon debating their own tendency to romanticize life before capitalism, the so-called "golden age" controversy. As they reopened questions of household production, early factory work, and the changing relation of women to property, meanwhile, women's historians helped to revitalize interest in the transition to capitalism among American historians generally. From the beginning, however, this work was primarily focused, not on questions of labor or the economy, but on ideology, and especially on the appearance of the amorphous cluster of ideas known as the cult of domesticity. Among the important early works were: Barbara Welter, "The Cult of True Womanhood 1820–1860," *American Quarterly*, 18 (Summer 1966), 151–74; Gerda Lerner, "The Lady and the Mill Girl: Changes in the Status of Women in the Age of Jackson," *Midcontinent American Studies Journal*, 10 (Spring 1969), 5–15; Kathryn Kish Sklar, *Catharine Beecher: A Study in American Domesticity* (New Haven, 1973); Thomas Dublin, "Women, Work, and the Family: Female Operatives in the Lowell Mills, 1830–1860," *Feminist Studies*, 3 (Fall 1975), 30–39; Dublin, *Women at Work*; Carroll Smith-Rosenberg, "The Female World of Love and Ritual," *Signs*, (Autumn 1975), 1–29; and Nancy F. Cott, *The Bonds of Womanhood: "Woman's" Sphere in New England, 1780–1835* (New Haven, 1977). Important examples of the debate over the "golden age" include Joan Hoff Wilson, "The Illusion of Change: Women and the American Revolution," in Alfred F. Young, ed., *The American Revolution: Explorations in the History of American Radicalism* (DeKalb, IL, 1976), 383–445; Mary Beth Norton, "The Myth of the Golden Age," in Carl R. Berkin and Mary Beth Norton, eds., *Women in America* (Boston, 1979), 37–47; and Gloria L. Main, "Widows in Rural Massachusetts on the Eve of the Revolution," in Ronald Hoffman and Peter J. Albert, eds., *Women in the Age of the American Revolution*, (Charlottesville, 1989), 67–90. For examples of early work in women's history that addressed questions of women's status before and after the transition to capitalism, see Ann D. Gordon and Mari Jo Buhle, "Sex and Class in Colonial and Nineteenth-Century America," in Berenice A. Carroll, ed., *Liberating Women's History: Theoretical and Critical Essays* (Urbana, 1976), 278–300; Heidi Hartmann, "Capitalism, Patriarchy, and Job Segregation by Sex," in Zillah R. Eisenstein, ed., *Capitalist Patriarchy and the Case for Socialist Feminism* (New York, 1979), 206–47; historical essays in Michelle Zimbalist Rosaldo and Louise

Lamphere, eds., *Woman, Culture, and Society* (Stanford, 1974); and Rayna R. Reitered., *Toward an Anthropology of Women* (New York, 1975).

5. See, for example, Mary P. Ryan, *Women in Public: Between Banners and Ballots, 1825–1880* (Baltimore, 1990); Edith B. Gelles, *Portia: The World of Abigail Adams* (Bloomington, 1992); Linda K. Kerber, "'I have Don . . . much to Carrey on the Warr': Women and the Shaping of Republican Ideology after the American Revolution," in Harriet B. Applewhite and Darline G. Levy, eds., *Women and Politics in the Age of the Democratic Revolution* (Ann Arbor, 1993), 227–58; and Rosemary Zagarri, *A Woman's Dilemma: Mercy Otis Warren and the American Revolution* (Wheeling, IL, 1995). Much of the debate over "republican motherhood" has remained centered almost exclusively in matters of political philosophy and ideology. See, for example, Kerber, *Women of the Republic*; Norton, *Liberty's Daughters*; and Jan Lewis, "The Republican Wife: Virtue and Seduction in the Early Republic," *William and Mary Quarterly*, 44 (Oct. 1987), 689–721.

6. For full citations on the literature of the transition to capitalism see note 4 in Gilje, "The Rise of Capitalism" in this volume.

7. Allan Kulikoff makes a distinction between "market" historians and "social" historians, placing, for example, Rothenberg and Henretta in the latter. See Kulikoff, "The Transition to Capitalism in Rural America," *William and Mary Quarterly*, 46 (Jan. 1989), 120–44.

8. Analyses of the emergence of "free labor," as either an economic system or an ideology, have been remarkably free of discussions of women's market activities. See, for example, Ronald Schultz, *The Republic of Labor: Philadelphia Artisans and the Politics of Class, 1720–1830* (New York, 1993); David Montgomery, *Citizen Worker: The Experience of Workers in the United States with Democracy and the Free Market during the Nineteenth Century* (New York, 1993); and Howard B. Rock, Paul A. Gilje, and Robert Asher, eds., *American Artisans: Crafting Social Identity, 1750–1850* (Baltimore, 1995).

9. For additional discussions of the gendered character of American labor history, see Ava Baron, "Gendered Subjects: Re-presenting 'The Worker' in History," paper presented at the Institute for Advanced Study, School of Social Science, March 10, 1994; and Alice Kessler-Harris, "Treating the Male as 'Other': Redefining the Parameters of Labor History," *Labor History*, 34 (Spring–Summer 1993), 190–204.

10. See, for example, Carole Shammas, "Black Women's Work and the Evolution of Plantation Society in Virginia," *Labor History*, 26 (Winter 1985), 5–28; Jacqueline Jones, "Race, Sex, and Self-Evident Truths: The Status of Women During the Era of the American Revolution" in Hoffman and Albert, eds., *Women in the Age of the American Revolution*, 293–337; and Barbara J. Fields, "Ideology and Race in American History," in J.

Morgan Kousser and James M. McPherson, eds., *Region, Race, and Reconstruction: Essays in Honor of C. Van Woodward* (New York, 1982),143–77. For recent work on "race" and the construction of the market, see esp. David R. Roediger, *The Wages of Whiteness: Race and the Making of the Working Class* (New York, 1991); Eric Foner, "Workers and Slavery," in Paul Buhle and Alan Dawley, eds., *Working for Democracy: American Workers from the Revolution to the Present* (Urbana, 1985) 21–30; Alexander Saxton, *The Rise and Fall of the White Republic: Class Politics and Mass Culture in Nineteenth-Century America* (New York, 1990); and Amy Dru Stanley, "Beggars Can't Be Choosers: Compulsion and Contract in Postbellum America," *Journal of American History,* 78 (March 1992), 1265–93.

11. The quotation is from Dublin, *Transforming Women's Work,* 8.

12. This summary of revolutionary-era economic conditions is based on John J. McCusker and Russell R. Menard, *The Economy of British America, 1607–1789* (Chapel Hill, 1985), esp. 351–77; James A. Henretta, "The War for Independence and American Economic Development," in Henretta, *The Origins of American Capitalism: Collected Essays* (Boston, 1991); Thomas M. Doerflinger, "Farmers and Dry Goods in the Philadelphia Market Area, 1750–1800," in Ronald Hoffman, John J. McCusker, Russell R. Menard, and Peter J. Albert, eds., *The Economy of Early America: The Revoluntionary Period, 1763–1790* (Charlottesville, 1988), 166–95; James A. Henretta, *The Origins of American Capitalism:Collected Essays* (Boston, 1991); Allan Kulikoff, *The Agrarian Origins of American Capitalism* (Charlottesville, 1992); Christopher Clark, *The Roots of Rural Capitalism: Western Massachusetts, 1780–1860* (Ithaca, 1990); Robert A. Gross, *The Minutemen and Their World* (New York, 1976); and Jean B. Lee, *The Price of Nationhood: The American Revolution in Charles County* (New York, 1994).

13. Daniel Vickers, "Competency and Competition: Economic Culture in Early America," *William and Mary Quarterly,* 47 (Jan. 1990), 4.

14. See, for example, *ibid.*; and Paul G. E. Clemens and Lucy Simler, "Rural Labor and the Farm Household In Chester County, Pennsylvania, 1750–1820," in Stephen Innes, ed., *Work and Labor in Early America* (Chapel Hill, 1988), 106–43.

15. Edith Abbott, *Women in Industry: A Study in American Economic History* (New York, 1910), 36–42; Blewett, *Men, Women, and Work,* 14. See also Blewett's "Work, Gender, and the Artisan Tradition in New England Shoemaking, 1760–1860," *Journal of Social History,* 17 (Winter 1983), 221–48; Susan Branson, "The Invisible Woman: The Family Economy in the Early Republic—The Case of Elizabeth Meredith," *Journal of the Early Republic,* 16 (Spring 1996), 47–71; Lois Green Carr and Lorena S. Walsh, "Economic Diversification and Labor Organization in the Chesapeake, 1650–1820," in Innes, *Work and Labor in Early America;* Faye E. Dudden,

Serving Women: Household Service in Nineteenth-Century America (Middletown, CT, 1983). Gloria Main argues that, in response to labor shortages, male employers began hiring larger numbers of women in the late colonial period; Main, "Gender, Work, and Wages in Colonial New England," *William and Mary Quarterly*, 51 (Jan. 1994), 64.

16. Toby L. Ditz, "Shipwrecked; or, Masculinity Imperiled: Mercantile Representations of Failure and the Gendered Self in Eighteenth-Century Philadelphia," *Journal of American History* 81 (June 1994), 51. For my related analysis of women's unpaid labor, see Jeanne Boydston, *Home and Work: Housework, Wages, and the Ideology of Labor in The Early Republic* (New York, 1990), chap. 3.

17. Daniel Vickers, "Competency and Competition," 9–10. For a discussion of the "deputy husband" role of women's prescribed labor, see Laurel Thatcher Ulrich, *Good Wives: Image and Reality in the Lives of Women in Northern New England* (New York, 1982), 36–50.

18. I have taken these examples from the Philadelphia City Directories for the 1790s and from the 1790 Philadelphia census. In both the cities and the country, the transition from "found labor to cash tenancy," that is, from the custom of receiving board and lodging as a part of one's compensation to the practice of purchasing room and board on the market, did not change the composition of women's household labor so much as it altered the relations of that labor. As Elizabeth Blackmar has noted, "In integrated household economies, the household head had claimed the authority of proprietor and employer as one. Within the market, boarders as purchasers could claim a status equal to that of seller." Formally, the new relations existed between the purchaser (the boarder) and the seller (the legal head of the household, usually the husband). But, as Blackmar's discussion of an argument between Thomas Paine and William Carver underscores, the new relations were likely to produce new tensions within the household, tensions articulated between the buyer and the provider of the services—the mistress: Paine's complaint was that Carver's wife had failed to make the bed, sweep the room, or serve his tea in a timely manner, or to direct her servant-woman to do so. Blackmar, *Manhattan for Rent, 1785–1850* (Ithaca, 1989), 63–64.

19. Stanley Elkins and Eric McKitrick, *The Age of Federalism: The Early American Republic, 1788–1800* (New York, 1993), 278.

20. Billy G. Smith, *The "Lower Sort": Philadelphia's Laboring People, 1750–1800* (Ithaca, 1990), 57–58, 108–25.

21. Kulikoff, "The Transition to Capitalism in Rural America," 137. Kulikoff's confidence on this point is the rule rather than the exception.

22. Carole Shammas, "Early American Women and Control over Capital" in Hoffman and Albert, eds., *Women in the Age of the American Revolu-*

tion, 134–54, esp. 140–47, 149. For a comparison with the Chesapeake region, see Lois Green Carr, "Inheritance in the Colonial Chesapeake," *ibid.,* 155–208. For additional studies of women and the law in the period of transition, see Norma Basch, *In the Eyes of the Law: Women, Marriage and Property in Nineteenth-Century New York* (Ithaca, 1982); Marylynn Salmon, *Women and the Law of Property in Early America* (Chapel Hill, 1986); and Richard H. Chused, *Private Acts in Public Places: A Social History of Divorce in the Formative Era of American Family Law* (Philadelphia, 1994), esp. chaps. 2 and 3.

23. Barbara Clark Smith, "Food Rioters and the American Revolution," *William and Mary Quarterly,* 51 (Jan. 1994), 5. For additional discussion of women in mobs during the revolutionary crisis, see Alfred F. Young, "The Women of Boston: 'Persons of Consequence' in the Making of the American Revolution, 1765–1776" in Harriet B. Applewhite and Darline G. Levy, eds., *Women and Politics in the Age of the Democratic Revolution* (Ann Arbor, 1990), 181–226. For a discussion of women in mobs in the postrevolutionary era, see Paul A. Gilje, *The Road to Mobocracy: Popular Disorder in New York City, 1763–1834* (Chapel Hill, 1987), esp. 85–91.

24. Kerber, *Women of the Republic,* 119–84; Norton, *Daughters of Liberty,* 228–55. I contrast my characterization of Ballard with James Henretta's emphasis on Ballard's life as an example of women working harder within the household in the postrevolutionary era. See Henretta, *The Origins of American Capitalism,* 267; and Laurel Thatcher Ulrich, *A Midwife's Tale: The Life of Martha Ballard, Based on Her Diary, 1785–1812* (New York, 1990).

25. Lisa Wilson Waciega, "A 'Man of Business': The Widow of Means in Southeastern Pennsylvania," *William and Mary Quarterly,* 44 (Jan. 1987), 40–64; and Branson, "The Invisible Woman." This attitude may also inform Nancy F. Cott's findings that both the total number of legal separations and the number of legal separations initiated by women increased in Massachusetts in the years after the Revolution. See Nancy F. Cott, "Eighteenth-Century Family and Social Life Revealed in Massachusetts Divorce Records," *Journal of Social History,* 10 (Fall 1976), 20–43.

26. For additional discussion of educated women in the late eighteenth century, see, for example, Zagarri, *A Woman's Dilemma;* Gelles, *Portia;* Lynne Withey, *Dearest Friend: A Life of Abigail Adams* (New York, 1981); Kerber, "'I Have Don ... much to Carrey on the Warr'"; Kerber, *Women of the Republic,* and Norton, *Daughters of Liberty.* On women's voluntary societies in the late eighteenth century, see, for example, Margaret Morris Haviland, "Beyond Women's Sphere: Young Quaker Women and the Veil of Charity in Philadelphia, 1790–1810," *William and Mary Quarterly,* 51 (July 1994), 419–46.

27. Abigail Adams to John Adams, July 31, [1777], in *The Book of*

Abigail and John: Selected Letters of the Adams Family, 1762–1784, ed. L. H. Butterfield, Marc Friedlander, and Mary-Jo Kline (Cambridge, MA, 1975), 184–85.

28. John Adams to Abigail Adams, Aug. 11, 1777, *ibid.*, 187; Gordon S. Wood, *The Creation of the American Republic, 1776–1787* (Chapel Hill, 1969), 319–21.

29. Vickers, "Competency and Competition," 26–27.

30. Ruth H. Bloch, "The Gendered Meanings of Virtue," *Signs*, 13 (Autumn 1987), 37–58. Mary Beth Norton, "Gender and Defamation in Seventeenth-Century Maryland," *William and Mary Quarterly*, 44 (Jan. 1987), 3–39. As Norton cautions, however, "The distinction between the all-male world and the world of heterosexual relations in seventeenth-century Maryland did not parallel the familiar modern division between public (male) and private (female) spheres. Rather, it delineated different aspects of the public sphere . . . in a society in which the modern concept of privacy would have been quite alien." (39) See Stansell, *City of Women*, 20–24, 90, on misogyny in the early republic.

31. John F. Watson, *Annals of Philadelphia and Pennsylvania in the Olden Time* (1830; 3 vols., rep., Philadelphia, 1899), I, 341–46. On "artisan republicanism," see Sean Wilentz, *Chants Democratic: New York City & the Rise of the American Working Class, 1788–1850* (New York, 1984), 61–103.

32. On the citizenship of females in the new republic, see Linda K. Kerber, "The Paradox of Women's Citizenship in the Early Republic: The Case of *Martin* v. *Massachusetts*, 1805," *American Historical Review*, 97 (Apr. 1992), 349–78; and Kerber, "A Constitutional Right to Be Treated Like American Ladies: Women and the Obligations of Citizenship," in Linda K. Kerber, Alice Kessler-Harris, and Kathryn Kish Sklar, eds., *U.S. History as Women's History: New Feminist Essays* (Chapel Hill, 1995), 17–35.

33. Peter Porcupine [William Cobbett], *A Kick for a Bite; or, Review Upon Review; with a Critical Essay, on the Works of Mrs. S. Rowson; in a Letter to the Editor, or Editors, of the American Monthly Review* (Philadelphia, 1795), 7, 12. For a further discussion of Cobbett's attack on Bache, see Susan Branson, "Politics and Gender: The Political Consciousness of Philadelphia Women in the 1790s" (Ph.D. diss., Northern Illinois University, 1992), 72. On the importance of literacy and publishing in the new "public" sphere, see Jurgen Habermas, *The Structural Transformation of the Public Sphere: An Inquiry into a Category of Bourgeois Society* (Cambridge, MA, 1989) 27–140. Compare with Mary Poovey, *Uneven Developments: The Ideological Work of Gender in Mid-Victorian England* (Chicago, 1988), esp. 1–23.

34. Thomas Branagan, *The Excellency of the Female Character Vindicated, Being an Investigation Relative to the Cause and Effects of the Encroach-*

ments of Men upon the Rights of Women, and the Too Frequent Degradation and Consequent Misfortunes of the Fair Sex (1807; 2d ed., Philadelphia, 1808), 26, 75. For a compatible analysis several decades later, see also Mary P. Ryan, *Women in Public: Between Ballots and Banners, 1825–1880* (Baltimore, 1990).

35. For a discussion of these terms in the later nineteenth century, see Ellen DuBois and Linda Gordon, "Seeking Ecstacy in the Battlefield: Pleasure and Danger in Nineteenth-Century Feminist Thought" in Carol Vance, ed., *Pleasure and Danger: Exploring Female Sexuality* (Boston, 1984), 7–25.

36. Ditz, "Representations of Failure and the Gendered Self," 63; John Barrell, "'The Dangerous Goddess': Masculinity, Prestige, and the Aesthetic in Early Eighteenth-Century Britain," *Cultural Critique*, 12 (Spring 1989), 124. The term "Public plainness" is from Kenneth J. E. Graham, *The Performance of Conviction: Plainness and Rhetoric in the Early English Renaissance* (Ithaca, 1994), see 1–24. See also Jay Fliegelman, *Declaring Independence: Jefferson, Natural Language, and the Culture of Performance* (Stanford, 1993).

37. Lerner, "The Lady and the Mill Girl." See also Stansell, *City of Women*, 193–216.

38. John Swanwick, *Thoughts on Education, Addressed to the Visitors of the Young Ladies' Academy in Philadelphia, October 31, 1787* (Philadelphia, 1787), 26.

39. The common construction of this point is that women were seeking their initial entry into civic life. I suspect that, more precisely, women who had exercised familial influence in the older paternalistic culture were seeking ways to replicate that power in the culture of the new republic "public sphere."

40. Mrs. [Susanna] Rowson, *Mentoria; or The Young Lady's Friend* (1791; 2 vols., Philadelphia, 1794), I, ii–iii.

41. I am indebted for this way of framing the impact of these changes to Rosemary Kegl, *The Rhetoric of Concealment: Figuring Gender and Class in Renaissance Literature* (Ithaca, 1994), 3.

THREE

Markets Without a Market Revolution: Southern Planters and Capitalism

DOUGLAS R. EGERTON

HISTORIANS, LIKE SOUTHERN ORATORS of other days, never tire of dueling over that historical perennial: the economic nature of the Old South. In recent decades, however, increased interest in market transformations has brought new attention to this enduring debate. Were the planters, as it is currently fashionable to suggest, calculating agrarian capitalists who operated their "factories in the field" according to commercial demand? Or were they, as the embattled minority continues to insist, unique and fundamentally prebourgeois seigneurial lords who participated in the capitalist Atlantic economy even as they resisted its values and ideology? Folly though it is to hope that scholars of the early republic will cease their often intemperate sparring over this issue, it may be possible to narrow the historiographical gulf by exposing as erroneous the current tendency to confuse capitalism and the market revolution. Few would dispute that large slaveholders participated in the Atlantic markets of the early nineteenth century and represented the agrarian wing of western capital. But unwaged labor blunted the influence of capitalism by advancing both a form of social relations and a premodern ideology that clashed with the competitive individualism and acquisitiveness that increasingly marked the capitalist North.[1]

There were some planters, it is true, for whom the notion of the slaveholder as businessman is most appropriate. If a "businessman" is interested in efficiency and maximum production in response to market demands, then virtually every master who produced for export could have fit the description. Production of all important staple crops rose and fell throughout the early national period in direct response to prices and orders. Tobacco planters in South Carolina, for example, who had adopted that staple during the mid-1780s, abandoned it with equal speed in favor of cotton when British factories posed lucrative new opportunities following the War of 1812, dramatic evidence of southern responsiveness to market signals.[2]

So, too, it is evident that market considerations helped to erode the harsh, hierarchical attitudes of the colonial seaboard South in the years after the Revolution, just as they did in the northern states. According to one popular interpretation, English patriarchalism metamorphosed not into planter seigneurialism but democratic entrepreneurship. Scots Irish immigrants in particular embraced the precepts of free enterprise and white egalitarianism. These petty slaveholders, unlike the less numerous great planters, regarded slavery as they did any other economic venture: the swiftest path to wealth and political power. Typical of their number was Abner Lawson Duncan of New Orleans, who dreamed of building an "elegant" estate, but instead poured his energies into creating a "profitable Plantation."[3]

Eager businessmen like Duncan undoubtedly responded to the economic changes that shook the Atlantic world following the peace treaties of Vienna and Ghent. The revival of textile production in Britain and the emergence of a foundling industrial order in the northeastern United States encouraged planters to devote their acreage to cotton. By 1820, southern states ginned 334,000 bales of cotton—up from 3000 in 1790—and by 1840, the number leaped to 1,350,000. Shrewd planters tramped ever westward for cheaper lands, much to the chagrin of those who remained on the eastern seaboard. "It is useless to seek to excite patriotic emotions in behalf of [their state] of birth," complained one Georgia planter, "when self-interest speaks so loudly." This new prosperity more than doubled the price of slaves and produced, by the eve of the Civil War, the republic's twelve richest counties. One cliometrician has gone so far to suggest that the South—even if separated from the North—constituted the world's fourth most prosperous nation by 1860.[4]

Despite the fact that most of this wealth was generated by unpaid chattel slaves, many scholars have concluded that planters were modern capitalists who found the transition to a free labor system after The War for Southern Independence surprisingly simple. Like all clever businessmen, one writer recently asserted, most slaveholders eagerly accepted government support in the name of economic development. South Carolina agriculturalists, for example, endorsed state subsidies for canals and other internal improvements that would improve the shipping of their commodities to northern urban centers.[5]

Market considerations also demanded an efficient allocation of labor, and the southern working class, like the men who owned it, could be highly mobile. Masters, not slaves, controlled both the division of labor within the family and the choice of crops each black family would produce, typically as part of a larger gang. When necessary—and too often it was believed to be—calculating southern businessmen dragged their slave families west, or broke them up by sale when a buyer with ready cash passed their gate. More than any other economic fact of life in the Old South, the internal slave trade demonstrated the often cruel demands of a voracious cotton market—as well as the limits of planter paternalism.[6]

Too many historians, however, have carelessly confused a commercial invasion with a capitalist revolution. Admittedly, no planter who kept one eye on Liverpool cotton prices could be totally free from the economic or social sway of Atlantic capitalism. But scholars who find capitalism triumphant in all corners of the early republic—and triumphant almost overnight, it would seem from some accounts—have paid far too much attention to the influence of markets on southern crop production. Those who would argue that the South was merely the North with whips and chains, should ponder the ways in which dominant southern social relations both kept a capitalist mentality at bay and hindered the growth of precisely those market mechanisms necessary for a well-rounded capitalist economy. More than simply an economic investment, slave labor provided the foundation for a premodern society that grew increasingly distinct from that of the northern Atlantic world as it continued to mature throughout the antebellum period. The need to discipline and defend unfree labor, in short, gave rise to a hierarchical society founded upon paternalism—an ongoing process of negotiation and violence that many scholars regrettably reduce to a simplistic model of accommodation—which produced an ideology linking whites and blacks with mutual responsibilities and obligations in a decidedly precapitalist relationship.[7]

Much of the current debate turns on the question of whether capitalism can exist when the majority of those who produce for the market are unpaid laborers who are owned by others. Recent studies of the market revolution in the North illustrate anew that *the* key ingredient in producing a robust capitalist economy above the Mason-Dixon was the rise of a fluid, free labor force, an ingredient notably absent in the South. If capitalism means nothing more than a simple desire for profit (no matter how small) or a mildly acquisitive mentality, virtually any landed elite in any century fits that modest description. But if capitalism is properly understood to be a series of social relations characterized by free-wage labor and the separation of the labor force from the means of production, so that labor is rendered incapable of subsisting without recourse to the market, then the slave South does not pass the test. Where the market mediated only the buying and selling of goods and not labor power—as was the case in the Old South—then it must be regarded as fundamentally dissimilar to conditions in the North.[8]

The emergence of a cash wage in place of a barter economy transformed commercial relations in the North, but this form of exchange was conspicuously absent in bargaining between master and slave. On the plantation, owner and laborer negotiated in the context of a harsh, premodern union not unlike that of lord and serf. The patriarchal relationship between the two, despite the fact that blacks were engaged in a form of exploitation designed to produce a profit for the master, was primarily social rather than economic. Relations of exchange between white planter and white factor may have been market-oriented, but relations of production between owner and worker manifestly were not.[9]

If paternal relations cannot easily be reconciled with the demands of capital, the same cannot be said of paternalism and the market economy. No fundamental conflict existed between white authoritarianism and the planters' need to remain solvent; rather it was just the opposite. Many Janus-faced slaveholders spoke two languages: that of profit with their factors, partners, and overseers, and that of paternalism with their laboring force. Henry Laurens of South Carolina, for example, permitted his slaves to "enjoy property" and barter with him for goods, but sought to contain the market within patriarchal confines by restricting his slaves' access to white shopkeepers. Seigneurial lords like Laurens rightly understood that forms of exchange outside his plantation—even those of a barter variety—damaged patriarchal control. He thus struggled to domesticate exchange by maintaining a monopoly on it, a form of manorial hegemony increasingly impossible to maintain in the early national North, where rural producers were liberated from compulsory obligations and dues. "Pray be so good as to give a watchful eye to the behaviour of Abraham & his gang," Laurens warned his overseer. "I will have no traffick carried on by them."[10]

When slaves could outwit such overseers and peddle food produced on their own provision grounds—small plots of land the bondpersons did not own but nonetheless claimed by traditional right—the informal, even underground economies they created hardly approximated the thriving cash-based networks appearing across the North. By the 1830s, enterprising merchants attracted northern producers to regional market days with slogans such as "cash for wool" and "wheat for cash." Northern consumerism and the demand for brand-name products helped transform the mentality of farmers and small town dwellers and hastened their acceptance of market capitalism. But in terms of individual spending in the South, all but the poorest whites enjoyed a greater disbursement power than the vast majority of slaves, who labored long and hard on Sundays and evenings for a meager financial reward.[11]

One should not, however, interpret the devastating poverty of the slaves to mean that slavery itself was unprofitable. As the modern advocates of a capitalist South never tire of remarking, some of the richest men in antebellum America were southern planters. That fact, however, hardly proves that slavery was a sound economic proposition for the South as a whole. Indeed, the question of whether slavery was profitable for some has little to do with whether it was a capitalist enterprise. Southern wealth was concentrated in very few hands, and even the richest planters could hardly consume enough local grain or craft goods to generate a healthy regional economy. Owning neither capital nor their persons, the forty percent of the southern population held as human property similarly bought little enough by comparison to their northern laboring counterparts. What scant property bondpersons were allowed to acquire was too paltry to sustain a southern manufacturing sector, and their legal status as chattel obviously meant that (unlike northern tenants) they lacked the ability to make the transition from landless laborers to profit-conscious yeomen farmers.[12]

Sheer optimism alone, a commodity most planter-politicians held in ample supply, was required to sustain the proposition that an independent South could be a wealthy country. The prosperity of a small number of white men was based solely on the export of an even smaller number of staple crops, most notably cotton. Southern prosperity thus was founded upon foreign consumption and the economic whims of an ever-fluctuating Atlantic market. Praying that the orders from English factories would never cease, southern politicians developed only those commercial institutions necessary to support an export-based economy. As the number of factories grew in New England and Britain, the South responded by plowing more acreage into production. In the cash-ready North, the demands of the market produced commercial agriculture, technological innovation, and an increasingly industrialized labor force. In the South, the demands of the market produced only more cotton—and more slave states.[13]

With southern capital tied up in land and slaves, the possibility that the market revolution would lead to a well-rounded economy with an industrial capitalist sector—as it had elsewhere in the republic—proved illusory. By the election of Andrew Jackson, slaveholders had invested nearly $30,000,000 in human property; a figure almost as vast as had been sunk into land. New England's merchant elite could subdivide profits enough to diversify into manufacturing; but unless a planter wished to liquidate his entire labor supply, neither his investment in land nor slaves could be reclaimed for industrial ventures. Understanding this situation all too well, export-minded slaveholders exhibited little interest in the entrepreneurial activity necessary for even small-scale manufacturing. "[H]owever true it is, as a general position, that domestic manufacturers is the true policy of nations," concluded Robert J. Turnbull of South Carolina, "as regards the application of the axiom [to] the plantation or cotton growing states, there is not one word of truth, in all that has been written as to the utility of manufactures."[14]

The economic realities of slavery, in fact, were always against those few urban dwellers who embraced the term capitalist. Industrialists there were in the South, but the laboring force that flocked toward factory towns in New England—farm women and immigrants—was nowhere to be found. Instead of moving toward southern urban centers, white artisans and unskilled workers fled to northern cities to escape the depressed wages caused by competition from slave hires. Immigrants devoutly wished to avoid slavery and slaves alike, and with the exception of New Orleans, remained outside the lower South. Foreign capital could not be attracted at any rate of interest. Defenders of southern industrial efforts today enjoy comparing the Old South's manufacturing ability to other western societies in post-colonial America, but that will hardly do. Southern whites compared their situation to the capitalist North, not to Colombia or Venezuela, and when they did so they found their own region sadly lacking. Slavery placed the South far "in the rear of our neighbors who are exempt from slavery," complained Henry Clay, "in the state of agriculture, the progress of manufacturers, the advance of improvement, and the general prosperity of society."[15]

For those determined to introduce manufacturing into the world of the slaveholders, only one possible source of industrial labor remained: the slaves. Rather to the surprise of southern industrialists, unfree workers hired out by their masters performed more than adequately, in part because canny manufacturers introduced such capitalist incentives as overtime pay into their operations. Yet slavery hindered the rise of industrial capitalism in a peculiar way. The prospect of semi-free wage slaves worried thoughtful slaveholders. Black workers at Virginia's Buffalo Forge put in extra hours to accumulate dangerously large sums on the credit side of their temporary owner's ledgers. Phill Easton, a master refiner, gained a balance of $100.28 by early 1840, far more cash than any paternalist thought a slave should possess. Worse yet, to maintain the complicated web of obligations central to plantation paternalism, slaveholders demanded adequate food and decent treatment for the slaves they hired out. When Robert Jemison of Alabama flogged one of the slaves in his cotton mill, the slave reported the abuse to his master, who sharply criticized Jemison's behavior. Industrial slavery was impossible "from views of proper discipline amongst Negroes," Jemison groused, "tending to spoil the Negroes to whom such privilege is granted and to corrupt others."[16]

Jemison's industrial slaves, however, had the ability to do what few other black southerners could do. They could afford to purchase manufactured goods and other household articles on the open market. Few southerners, black or white, patronized home industries, and indeed, few cared to. One of the large plantation's greatest assets—its ability to achieve maximum labor efficiency through the forced allocation of diversified labor—meant that it required little in the way of manufactured goods from the outside world. Grand plantations were judged not only by the number of bales they ginned, but also by the skill of their slave seamstresses and the artistic ability of their blacksmiths. As a result, all but the biggest manufacturing operations struggled against the indifference of southern consumers, who in any case tended to regard southern products as inferior to northern or European articles.[17]

If masters and slaves were indifferent consumers, another significant segment of the southern population was equally so. Beside the market-oriented great manor stood the family farm. Owning few or no slaves and producing nothing for export, the upcountry yeomen remained on the periphery of the market economy throughout the antebellum period. Far more common, if far less influential, than their wealthy neighbors, the fiercely independent farmers practiced diversified farming for household subsistence and neighborhood exchange. It makes little sense, of course, to attribute the retention of such precapitalist types of agriculture to the influence of slavery, unless it can be demonstrated that such practices were independent of the great planters' successful efforts to monopolize the market and keep bourgeois values at bay. But can we believe otherwise? Whereas in the North the availability of credit and banking facilities fueled a revolution in market agriculture and consumer attitudes, most southern yeomen remained far removed from the capitalist tentacles of the Atlantic economy. Richard Medlin, a North Carolina farmer, recalled late in life that his mother "spun and wove every piece of their clothing from cotton and wool they had raised." The shoes he wore were sewn by his father "from home-grown materials."[18]

If the southern yeoman farmer finished the season with a surplus of corn and hogs, the balance would be bartered at a nearby country store. Although local merchants preferred payment in hard currency, most exchanged their sugar, coffee, shoes, and hats for food crops. But the amounts traded—often less than ten dollars a year—were too little to either draw the yeomen into the market economy or help support southern manufacture. (Most of the finished goods traded at country stores came from the North.) Farmers regarded cash as they did corn, as a practical tool for exchange, but rarely as something to be acquired for itself. Influenced by the patrician demeanor of their wealthy neighbors, with whom they occasionally traded corn or pork, the yeomen exhibited neither an interest in nor an understanding of the acquisitive, entrepreneurial instincts of northern farmers. The country store and the larger world it represented served their interests well enough, but it did not dominate them.[19]

Even those southern yeomen who settled in the Old Northwest carried their tradition-bound, subsistence forms of agriculture with them. Old practices died slowly, and old customs died harder still. Most transplanted farmers continued to raise corn and hogs in an attempt to retain their distinctive, noncapitalist way of life. Hogs and cattle provided their families with food, but more importantly, accorded them a great deal of leisure time. Agrarians who emigrated from New England, however, demonstrated the compulsive pursuit of wealth typical of northern commercial agriculture by growing a wheat and other cereal crops, most of which were intended for sale at urban markets.[20]

Somewhat more intent on maximizing profit, but little more interested in challenging premodern labor patterns, the yeomen's planter brethren also discovered that a society based on slavery resisted all attempts at economic modernization. Proslavery writers devoted column after column in newspapers and periodicals to theories of horticultural reform. But rendering unfree labor more efficient was no easy task, and planter polemicists knew it. South Carolina Senator James Henry Hammond, for example, accepted the theory of diversification of plantation production but found that the crops, equipment, and animals available to him were limited by his determination to become more efficient using unpaid labor. After years of frustration and failure, Hammond, like most Lower South agriculturalists, abandoned his dreams of introducing capitalist elements into a premodern mode of production and fought to earn even a meager profit by simply expanding the amount of acreage his slow-moving workers planted.[21]

Despite, or perhaps because of such failures, planter intellectuals frequently lashed out at their more prosperous free-state competitors. Insisting that northern "wage slaves" enjoyed little more than the right to starve while searching for temporary employment, southerners contrasted their seigneurial community with the alleged benefits of free market capitalism. One pamphleteer claimed that wage work constituted "the most intolerable slavery that men can suffer." Where black "servants" possessed the love and protection of their white master, the northern workers "were liable to have that employment [terminated] at any moment, either by caprice, ill health, or the state of trade." Many scholars tend to dismiss such tirades as deceitful and hypocritical replies to northern abolitionists. But in doing so they underestimate the extent to which planters labored to rebuild a world of organic relations of dependency and mutuality. The anticapitalist sentiments routinely expressed by Thomas Dew, George Fitzhugh, and John C. Calhoun were the logical product of their society's fundamentally premodern relationship between the ownership and means of production, that is, between the master and the slave.[22]

Not content merely to criticize the theoretical mechanisms necessary to drive a capitalist market economy, such as a mobile working class and a healthy market for manufactured goods, the southern elite habitually denounced those commercial facilities that threatened to carry their region into a new stage of economic development. It was not that they failed to grasp fully the critical connection between banking and internal improvements in bringing about economic change in the rest of the nation, but rather that they understood all too well that a transportation revolution allowed for the infusion of ideas antithetical to their seigneurial outlook. Modern writers enamored of the theory of a probusiness South have discovered broad support for internal improvements, but that would come as bewildering news to the handful of frustrated southern Whigs who pushed for roads and canals. Slaveholders were notoriously concerned with growing federal power, and dogmatic planters based their objections to national funding for roads and canals on constitutional theories inspired by their determination to protect slavery. Robert Turnbull, for one, demanded an end to "appropriations for Canals and other National works, which are drawing the life blood of the South," but other southern politicians revealed the true source of their worries. If "Congress can make canals," warned Nathaniel Macon, "they can with more propriety emancipate."[23]

Whatever the source of their anxiety, planter statesmen typically barred the path to regional economic development. All too often, state plans for internal improvements fared little better. Although no constitutional scruples stood in the way of state appropriations, few penurious tidewater planters wished to pay the state taxes or tolls necessary for the construction of upland roads they would never use. Robert Barnwell Rhett consequently relied on the argument that as the South had no true interests but agriculture, any expenditure of scant resources on turnpikes or other improved transportation facilities amounted to a "tax" designed to "oppress us for the enrichment of the manufacturers."[24]

If the Atlantic market shaped the plantation economy to its own ends, it simultaneously spawned a landed elite with economic interests and moral values antagonistic to the spirit of modern capitalism. Those who would characterize antebellum slavery as capitalism have shown us markets, but no revolution, profits, but no regional prosperity, and capital, but no capitalists. Such a theory leaves unanswered why the agrarian capitalists of the South, who presumably spoke the language of maximum profit, found it impossible to come to terms with the industrial capitalists of the North, or to follow free labor advocates down their path to greater prosperity. But Robert Turnbull knew the answer. The "time would come," he warned, "when the surplus capital of the Northern and Middle States might be profitably employed in Manufacturers, [and] would promote their local interests at the expense and ruin of the

Southern States" and their peculiar institutions. The only option would be disunion. Turnbull was long dead when the day he prophesied came, but he would hardly have been displeased at the tragic decision his sons made.

NOTES

1. I have been especially influenced on this point by Michael Merrill, "Putting 'Capitalism' in Its Place: A Review of Recent Literature," *William and Mary Quarterly*, 52 (April 1995), 315–26, who reminds us that if "capitalism is little more than a synonym for the market economy, then any opposition to capitalism necessarily becomes an opposition to markets" (317). The plantation South obviously did not exhibit such opposition. Peter Kolchin, *American Slavery, 1619–1877* (New York, 1993), 170, contains a succinct description of the nature of the current debate.

2. This view has been most systematically advanced by Robert Fogel and Stanley Engerman, *Time on the Cross: The Economics of American Negro Slavery* (2 vols., Boston, 1974), and, with some modification, again by Robert Fogel, *Without Consent or Contract: The Rise and Fall of American Slavery* (New York, 1989), 64–65, who calls slavery "a flexible, highly developed form of capitalism." Edward Pessen, "How Different from Each Other Were the Antebellum North and South?" *American Historical Review*, 85 (Oct. 1980), 1119–49, also disparaged the theory of southern distinctiveness by suggesting that whatever their economic interests, southern whites lived much as did northern whites, in a stratified society marked by inequalities in status, material condition, and opportunity. The same could be said, of course, for any society at any time and at any place on the globe.

3. James Oakes, *The Ruling Race: A History of American Slaveholders* (New York, 1982), xii–xiii, 25; Abner Lawson Duncan to Andrew Jackson, April 23, 1816, in *The Papers of Andrew Jackson*, ed. Sam B. Smith *et al.* (Knoxville, 1980–), IV, 23–24. Barrington Moore, Jr., *Social Origins of Dictatorship and Democracy: Lord and Peasant in the Making of the Modern World* (Boston, 1966), also argues that the plantation South presented a unique variety of capitalism, although unlike Oakes, Moore suggests that most slaveholders rejected liberal conceptions of democracy and equality of opportunity. Peter J. Parish, *Slavery: History and Historians* (New York, 1989), 52, provides an incisive critique of Oakes's provocative thesis.

4. Fogel, *Without Consent or Contract*, 87; Charles G. Sellers, *The Mar-*

ket Revolution: Jacksonian America, 1815–1846 (New York, 1991), 407–08 (quotation).

5. Laurence Shore, *Southern Capitalists: The Ideological Leadership of an Elite, 1832–1885* (Chapel Hill, 1986), xii; Shearer Davis Bowman, *Masters and Lords: Mid-19th Century U.S. Planters and Prussian Junkers* (New York, 1993), 95–97.

6. Gavin Wright, *The Political Economy of the Cotton South: Households, Markets, and Wealth in the Nineteenth Century* (New York, 1978), 87; Michael Tadman, *Speculators and Slaves: Masters, Traders, and Slaves in the Old South* (Madison, 1989), 218.

7. The view that unfree labor produced a nonmarket *society* fundamentally different from that of the capitalist North can be found in the complicated and sophisticated writings of Eugene D. Genovese, especially *The World the Slaveholders Made: Two Essays in Interpretation* (New York, 1969); Genovese, *In Red and Black: Marxian Explorations in Southern and Afro-American History* (New York, 1968); Genovese, *Roll, Jordan, Roll: The World the Slaves Made* (New York, 1974); and, Genovese and Elizabeth Fox-Genovese, *Fruits of Merchant Capital: Slavery and Bourgeois Property in the Rise and Expansion of Capitalism* (New York, 1983). One should also consult Alan Gallay, "The Origins of Slaveholders' Paternalism: George Whitefield, the Bryan Family, and the Great Awakening in the South," *Journal of Southern History*, 53 (Aug. 1987), 371, for the critical background of the eighteenth century; and Philip Morgan, "Three Planters and Their Slaves: Perspectives on Slavery in Virginia, South Carolina, and Jamaica, 1750–1790," in Winthrop D. Jordan and Sheila Skemp, eds., *Race and Family in the Colonial South: Essays* (Jackson, MS, 1987), 39–40, on the shift from patriarchalism to paternalism.

8. Merrill, "Putting 'Capitalism' in Its Place," 326; Steven Hahn, "Capitalists All!" *Reviews in American History*, 11 (June 1983), 222–23; Edward L. Ayers, "The World the Liberal Capitalists Made," *Reviews in American History*, 19 (June 1991), 198.

9. Peter Kolchin, *Unfree Labor: American Slavery and Russian Serfdom* (Cambridge, MA, 1987), 360. Even James Oakes, the most articulate advocate of antebellum slavery as a form of capitalism, concedes that "master and slave formed what was, at bottom, a nonmarket relationship." See Oakes, *Slavery and Freedom: An Interpretation of the Old South* (New York, 1990), 54.

10. Robert Olwell, "'A Reckoning of Accounts': Patriarchy, Market Relations, and Control on Henry Laurens's Lowcountry Plantations, 1762–1785," in Larry E. Hudson, Jr., ed., *Working Toward Freedom: Slave Society and Domestic Economy in the American South* (Rochester, 1994), 33–52; Henry Laurens to John Smith, Sept. 5, 1765, in *The Papers of Henry Laurens,*

ed. Philip M. Hamer, *et al.* (Columbia, S.C., 1968–), V, 2–3. Even Robert Fogel has conceded that "there need be no overriding conflict between paternal attitudes and the desire to make money." See Fogel, "The Southern Slave Economy," in Harry P. Owens, ed., *Perspectives and Irony in American Slavery: Essays* (Jackson, 1976), 86–87.

11. Roderick A. McDonald, *The Economy and Material Culture of Slaves: Goods and Chattels on the Sugar Plantations of Jamaica and Louisiana* (Baton Rouge, 1993), 52–57; Betty Wood, *Women's Work, Men's Work: The Informal Slave Economies of Lowcountry Georgia* (Athens, 1995), 131–32. See Andrew R. L. Cayton and Peter S. Onuf, *The Midwest and the Nation: Rethinking the History of an American Region* (Bloomington, 1990), 116, on consumerism in the Old Northwest; and Mary P. Ryan, *Cradle of the Middle Class: The Family in Oneida County, New York, 1790–1865* (Cambridge, 1981), 9, on the growing importance of cash to the northern countryside. From bank president to saloonkeeper, Ryan observes, "the only economic term more popular than 'capital' was the word 'cash.'" Few southerners of either race, by contrast, applied to themselves either this definition of capitalist or the earlier definition of Adam Smith, that is, an investor with a great deal of surplus capital to invest in a variety of enterprises.

12. Parish, *Slavery*, 55–56. This is not to say that there were no slaveholding capitalists in the broad, diverse South, but rather than they were the exception and not the rule. Certainly running a sugar plantation required a great deal of capital. A sugar mill with its steam engine coast upward of $40,000, and the southern Whigs who owned these agricultural factories were businessmen in the northern sense. See Clement Eaton, *The Growth of Southern Civilization, 1790–1860* (New York, 1961), chap. 6; and J. Carlyle Sitterson, *Sugar Country: The Cane Sugar Industry in the South, 1753–1950* (Lexington, 1953), chap. 2. For those who wish to wade into the debate on slavery's profitability, Harold D. Woodman, "The Profitability of Slavery: A Historical Perennial," *Journal of Southern History*, 29 (Aug. 1963), 303–25, is a good place to start.

13. Drew Gilpin Faust, "The Rhetoric and Ritual of Agriculture in Antebellum South Carolina," *Journal of Southern History*, 45 (Nov. 1979), 541–68. Kolchin, *American Slavery*, 174, suggests that southern wealth, "like that of modern Saudi Arabia, was based on the fortuitous ability to export ever-increasing quantities of a highly prized commodity, but did not indicate a developed economy."

14. Charles M. Wiltse, *John C. Calhoun: Nationalist, 1782–1828* (Indianapolis, 1944), 376–77; Wright, *Political Economy of the Cotton South*, 8, 126; [Robert J. Turnbull], *The Crisis: Or, Essays on the Usurpation of the federal government* (Charleston, 1827), 113. Most—but certainly not all—critics of the precapitalist model concede that slave labor hindered the

rise of a healthy industrial sector, but nonetheless insist that the South was an example of pure agrarian capitalism. But what other modern agrarian society failed to make the qualitative leap to manufacturing? The answer must remain that continued reliance upon unfree labor and staple production reduced the South to a colony of regions and countries with diversified, capitalist economies.

15. Wright, *Political Economy of the Cotton South*, 120–23; Henry Clay to the Colonization Society of Kentucky, Dec. 17, 1829, in *The Papers of Henry Clay*, ed. James. F. Hopkins, Robert Seager *et al.* (11 vols., Lexington, 1959–1992), VIII, 142.

16. Daniel Walker Howe, *The Political Culture of the American Whigs* (Chicago, 1979), 133; Charles B. Dew, *Bond of Iron: Master and Slave at Buffalo Forge* (New York, 1994), 114–15; Randall Miller, "The Fabric of Control: Slavery in Antebellum Southern Textile Mills," *Business History Review*, 55 (Winter 1981), 487.

17. Ralph V. Anderson and Robert E. Gallman, "Slaves as Fixed Capital: Slave Labor and Southern Economic Development," *Journal of American History*, 64 (June 1977), 39; Eugene D. Genovese, "The Significance of the Slave Plantation for Southern Economic Development," *Journal of Southern History*, 28 (Nov. 1962), 425.

18. Steven Hahn, *The Roots of Southern Populism: Yeoman Farmers and the Transformation of the Georgia Upcountry, 1850–1890* (New York, 1983), 4; Bill Cecil-Fronsman, *Common Whites: Class and Culture in Antebellum North Carolina* (Lexington, 1992), 98–99, 103; Michael Merrill, "Cash Is Good to Eat: Self Sufficiency and Exchange in the Rural Economy of the United States," *Radical History Review*, 15 (Winter, 1977), 42–71; John Boles, *The South Through Time: A History of an American Region* (Englewood Cliffs, 1995), 184–86.

19. Hahn, *Roots of Southern Populism*, 32–39; Donald L. Winters, *Tennessee Farming, Tennessee Farmers: Antebellum Agriculture in the Upper South* (Knoxville, 1994), 49–51; Michael Merrill, "So What's Wrong With the 'Household Mode of Production'?" *Radical History Review*, 22 (Spring 1979), 141–46. For full citations of the literature of the transition to capitalism, including the northern countryside, see note 4 in Paul A. Gilje, "The Rise of Capitalism," in this volume.

20. Cayton and Onuf, *Midwest and the Nation*, 40–42.

21. Eugene D. Genovese, *The Political Economy of Slavery: Studies in the Economy and Society of the Slave South* (New York, 1965), 124–31; Drew Gilpin Faust, *James Henry Hammond and the Old South: A Design for Mastery* (Baton Rouge, 1982), chap. 6. David F. Allmendinger, Jr., "The Early Career of Edmund Ruffin, 1810–1840," *Virginia Magazine of History and Biography*, 93 (Apr. 1985), 127–54, purports to prove that agricultural re-

form was possible within the context of slavery and should be read with skepticism.

22. Kenneth Greenberg, *Masters and Slaves: The Political Culture of American Slavery* (Baltimore, 1985), 100; C. Vann Woodward, "A Southern War Against Capitalism," in *American Counterpoint: Slavery and Racism in the North-South Dialogue* (Boston, 1971), 107–39; Eric Foner, *Free Soil, Free Labor, Free Men: The Ideology of the Republican Party Before the Civil War* (1970; 2d ed., New York, 1995), xviii–xix.

23. [Turnbull], *The Crisis*, 37–38; quoted in Harry L. Watson, *Jacksonian Politics and Community Conflict: The Emergence of the Second American Party System in Cumberland County, North Carolina* (Baton Rouge, 1981), 51.

24. Thomas E. Jeffrey, *State Parties and National Politics: North Carolina, 1815–1861* (Athens, 1989), 123; Charleston (SC) *Mercury*, April 24, 1830.

25. [Turnbull], *The Crisis*, 20.

FOUR

Rural America and the Transition to Capitalism

CHRISTOPHER CLARK

IT IS NO ACCIDENT THAT STUDIES OF RURAL HISTORY have been central to the recent debate over the emergence of commercial, industrial, and agrarian capitalism in America from the seventeenth to the nineteenth centuries. For one thing, rural people made up a majority of the population throughout the period, and until the 1880s agriculture employed a majority of the U.S. workforce. Through the Civil War, too, agricultural goods provided both a preponderance of U.S. export earnings and the raw materials for the largest American industries. Historians have long recognized these facts, but a set of conceptual changes over the last two decades has led to a reevaluation of the rural contribution to American history. On one hand there has been a recognition that economic activities were profoundly influenced by social and cultural factors; on the other, the view that rural societies were not simply passive victims of change imposed from outside but could have a significant influence on the patterns of change themselves. Processes such as industrialization and urbanization did not just spread from towns into the countryside but also found their roots there, in the variety of rural societies that early America produced.[1]

I have argued elsewhere that capitalism is defined, not by the existence of any one set of practices or institutions, but by the accretion over time of a whole range of them. These may briefly be summarized under three headings: first, what Max Weber called the "spirit" of capitalism, including the aspiration to accumulate and use material goods for investment in future activities for profit, and the institution of rational means for calculating to that end; second, a prominent role for markets in regulating major economic activity, especially the exchange of goods; and third, the emergence of "free" wage labor based on the creation of markets in labor power. An evolved capitalist economy may be said to be one in which all three of these aspects coincide and in which the pursuit of profit and the use of markets and wage labor characterize most economic relationships most of the time. Historians continue to debate when the U.S. economy acquired these characteristics, but there is increasing acceptance that they did not together become dominant until the nineteenth century. In what follows I shall identify aspects of American rural society that were critical to their emergence.[2]

The connections between rural societies and the evolution of commercial and industrial capitalism were not straightforward. Early America had clear capitalist roots in the trading companies of early modern Europe and the growing Atlantic commercial world. But the actual processes of settlement introduced pressures that placed rural Americans in ambiguous relationships with that world. The conquest and occupation of Native American territory and the consequent high land-to-labor ratio confronting white settlers drew many of them, with their practices and aspirations, away from the commercial milieu and towards the hope of more independent livelihoods of their own. Though only a minority were completely disconnected from the need to calculate, accumulate, and participate to some degree in market transactions, most early rural Americans removed themselves from capitalist social relations. Not all relied predominantly on markets and few entirely relied for their livelihoods either on hiring labor or doing hired work themselves.

This tension between independence and capitalism continued throughout the period of this discussion, but changes in the eighteenth and nineteenth centuries significantly altered rural peoples' connections with wider economic processes. Recent research and writing makes it possible to map the outlines of the rural role in the emergence of American capitalism: the contribution, on one hand, of rural societies to overall capitalist development; and the ambiguous emergence, on the other, of capitalist relationships in parts of the American countryside itself. These relationships, in turn, rested on the evolution of patterns of market involvement among rural producers and on the creation of markets for rural wage labor. But these changes took different forms and occurred to differing extents, and the task of mapping them is impossible without recognizing significant regional differences and chronological shifts. Though important variations occurred within them, it is useful to divide early America into four regions—the South, the mid-Atlantic, New England, and the trans-Appalachian West— and to consider two main periods: the years up to and those following the American Revolution.[3]

In colonial North America, as in many other regions of European colonization, the high ratio of available land to available labor severely restrained the emergence of farming based on permanent wage labor of the kind that grew up in seventeenth- and eighteenth-century England and some other European regions.[4] Agriculture relied instead on forms of dependent or coerced labor, and two broadly contrasting kinds of agricultural society emerged during the seventeenth and eighteenth centuries. Present throughout the colonies, but dominating New England and parts of the mid-Atlantic region, were small and modest-sized farms primarily reliant on family labor, many of which sought to produce or trade locally for most of their subsistence needs but raised a portion of their crops for market sale in order to purchase necessities and pay taxes. Primarily in the mid-Atlantic region and especially in the South, were farms concerned mainly with growing staple crops for export markets, using the labor of indentured servants or slaves. In localities such as the Hudson River Valley and parts of the Chesapeake, where land grants had led to the creation of large agricultural estates, tenant farming also grew up.[5]

The type of labor used could depend on the characteristics of major crops, their growing cycles, and the intensity of work required to tend and harvest them. In parts of the Chesapeake that switched from tobacco to grain cultivation from the mid-eighteenth century, tenants and hired hands started to displace slaves.[6] But cultural and social-structural considerations could also shape variations in the agricultural labor force. Wheat cultivation expanded rapidly in eighteenth-century Pennsylvania, but whereas German-speaking farmers most commonly used family labor, English-speaking districts came to rely more heavily on indentured servants and smallholding, tenant "inmates." In that they produced significant commercial crops making heavy use of formally free laborers, these latter wheat farming areas came closer than any part of rural America up to the late-eighteenth century to matching the criteria for agrarian capitalism.[7]

The majority of American farmers, however, were "yeomen" owners or at least tenants of the land they tilled, users of family and locally exchanged labor who, as Allan Kulikoff has pointed out, balanced their involvement in market production with fulfilling the needs of their households from resources they could, in some measure, control.[8] The pursuit of household "independence," while it rarely produced literal self-sufficiency, strongly influenced rural culture, farming practices, and attitudes toward land and accumulation. In New England and in many upcountry regions elsewhere, there was a substantial degree of local self-sufficiency and poor integration with distant, international markets. Accounting practices were devoted to keeping track of local debts and credits, not to calculating profits. Land acquisition and migration patterns were shaped by families' needs to accumulate property to support succeeding generations from the land, and to recreate a degree of household independence for them if possible. As settlement in eastern regions became completed during the eighteenth century and population pressed on available land resources the ideal of agrarian independence began to change the course of American politics and history.[9]

Pressure on land was far from being the only cause of the American Revolution, but demands for westward expansion and the activities of land speculators eager to profit by it helped shape the political conflict with Britain. The constitutional settlement that emerged from America's independence from Britain embodied dreams of an agrarian republic. The Revolution helped guarantee the conquest and subsequent settlement of the trans-Appalachian West in the late eighteenth and nineteenth centuries, a process influenced by the extension of the yeoman ideal.[10] Had this ideal alone determined the realities, then North America might for a considerable period have developed along noncapitalist lines, as household production and the extensive employment of family labor restrained the accumulation of commercial centers and a wage-earning labor force. To some extent, that is what did happen, as farmers and hunters spread across the landscape. But other factors were also at work to ensure that, even as it was being created, the agrarian republic would be turned in new directions. Strong regional distinctions based on the character of rural societies would, however, still remain significant after the Revolution, as they had in the colonial period.

Property owners were proportionately more numerous among the early U.S. population than in any contemporary European society, and markedly more so than in some. Nevertheless, property- and wealth-holding in the new republic was unequal. Lee Soltow has calculated that even among free adult males, the group that possessed most of the nation's property, only just under half owned any land in 1798 and that, although there were marked regional variations, nowhere was land equally distributed. These inequalities would have a marked effect on the patterns of emergence of American capitalism in the decades following the Revolution, often in ways that at first sight appear paradoxical.[11]

The South, the region already most heavily engaged in staple-crop production for market, increased this commitment markedly in the late eighteenth and early nineteenth centuries, particularly with the rapid expansion of cotton cultivation and of settlement across the deep South and Southwest. By 1860 cotton alone provided three-fifths of U.S. exports by value. This was mainly achieved, of course, by the extension of plantation slavery, so market agriculture in the South rested predominantly on non-capitalist social relations. The number of yeoman farm families in the South also grew; in some places they pioneered new settlements for staple-crop production but were then frequently pushed aside by slave plantations. Yeomen remained dominant mainly in upland or marginal areas where links to distant markets were weak. The provisions of game laws and the preservation of the open range for grazing in much of the antebellum South enabled yeoman families to supplement their own crops with the products of hunting and livestock. Even those who increased their output of cash-earning cotton or grain crops continued sufficient subsistence production to retain at least some shelter from markets.[12]

Though the matter is still much debated, there is an emerging agreement among historians of slavery that although the plantation system superficially resembled capitalist agriculture there were important social, cultural and ideological distinctions between owning labor and hiring labor-power that made slavery non-capitalist in character. Planters' political power, their commitment to investing in slaves, and their increasing reluctance during the antebellum period to countenance relaxations of the slave regime, significantly restrained them from making diversified investments in commerce, infrastructure, and manufacturing. Such flexible reallocation of labor or capital might have placed their control over slave labor at risk. As James Oakes has recently pointed out, most slaveholders were by the middle of the nineteenth century so far from viewing their slave property simply as assets exchangeable in the marketplace that they refused even to contemplate proposals for compensated emancipation. Urban, industrial, and transport developments consequently proceeded at a slower rate in the South than in other regions. Another recent study has shown that the one-third or one-half of the southern white population who owned no property, and were consequently available for paid employment, usually labored in marginal and seasonal jobs rather than obtaining permanent, full-time work.[13]

Because of slavery the plantation South remained the only major part of the U.S. in which large landholders became directly involved in farming, controlling the labor that large-scale agriculture required and reaping the profits. In nonslave regions assembling, controlling and retaining labor on such a scale was difficult or impossible. Family labor was insufficient for large-scale farming; indentured servitude and other forms of dependent labor were declining by the end of the eighteenth century. Under conditions of land abundance wage labor would be expensive and hard to retain, except in special circumstances, so the emergence of agrarian capitalism as such was restrained. Most regions outside the plantation South came to be dominated by modest-sized farms; relatively few holdings were directly worked on a scale larger than most farm families (often with the small-scale or seasonal assistance of hired help) could manage. But developments in three main regions—the mid-Atlantic, New England, and the West—between the Revolution and the Civil War indicate that it was these small-farming regions that, paradoxically, gave most impetus to the development of commercial and industrial capitalism. Rural societies provided the basis for the emergence of commercial networks and infrastructure and helped provide a wage labor force for new manufactures. These arrangements also drew farmers away from independence towards new commercial and social relationships.

Agricultural systems provided part of the basis for the industrial transformation of the mid-Atlantic region and New England from the late eighteenth century onwards, but in different ways according to circumstances. In southeastern Pennsylvania, which had absorbed large numbers of European immigrants as servants and laborers, population growth and the strong seasonal fluctuations in work required for wheat cultivation created a large group of relatively poor and unattached workers easily attracted to alternative employment, particularly as international wheat markets stagnated from the 1790s on. Added to a continued flow of European immigrants, this rural surplus labor force (much of it male) formed the basis for the rapid growth of textile and other manufactures in rural hamlets and mill villages, and particularly in the Philadelphia area itself, that created one of America's first industrial regions.[14]

New England agriculture, largely devoted to nonstaple, diversified production using family labor and intermittent hired help, contributed to early industrial development by different means. Without the fluctuating labor demands of wheat raising, and relatively unattractive to European immigrants, late-eighteenth century New England had fewer obvious sources of surplus rural labor than the mid-Atlantic region, except on the coast, where the fishing industry had created pockets of impoverished workers. Still, population pressure on land and the preexisting diversity of skills in a small-farm economy encouraged increasing levels of manufacturing output. This development occurred at first largely in rural households, as people sought to put together livelihoods that they could no longer secure from farming alone. This process, coupled with shifting gender divisions of labor in farm households, created over the early nineteenth century opportunities for entrepreneurs to draw rural labor (in this case, much of it female) into manufacturing. The textile mills of the "Rhode Island" or "family" system set up in southern New England from the 1790s onwards, the large mills of the Waltham-Lowell system that attracted many thousands of young rural women to work away from home between the 1810s and 1840s, and rural-based manufacturing outwork of different kinds, each in distinct ways tapped the labor of an agricultural economy that was undergoing a steady but subtle process of demographic change and commercialization.[15]

These industries recruited women workers to a greater extent than in the mid-Atlantic region partly because surplus male labor was scarce in the New England countryside. But the pattern of labor recruitment was also influenced throughout the Northeast by wealth distribution and ease of access to landholding. Prominent among the shifts in late eighteenth- and early nineteenth-century farming was a decline in household-based textile production. Depending on family resources and local circumstances different activities emerged to substitute for this. Many comfortable or prosperous farm families increased their dairying output, as their women devoted the considerable effort required to produce cheese or butter for market sale and so achieved for themselves a measure of independence within the household system.[16] Other families, many of them poorer, came to rely on taking in manufacturing outwork from local merchants. The spread of outwork systems in different trades across New England also followed patterns rooted in circumstances. In eastern Massachusetts and New Hampshire, where population pressure on land was greatest, large numbers of rural women worked for shoe merchants and manufacturers based in centers such as Lynn, Haverhill, and Walpole, Massachusetts. In upland and inland regions, where demographic pressure was slighter and livelihoods from farming still viable, women took in work on buttons, straw- or palm-leaf hats whose production could be accommodated to the other rhythms of household work. Rural outwork, however, was generally much more significant in New England than it was in the mid-Atlantic region. This was in part a consequence of the higher average prosperity of mid-Atlantic farm-owning families, who were proportionately more likely than their New England counterparts to rely on dairy production for outside income. Relative prosperity, therefore, enabled farm families to hold themselves aloof from the industrial labor market even as they contributed to growing produce markets. The mid-Atlantic region saw a more rapid, firmer distinction between middle-class farm families and permanent industrial workers than did rural New England where, for much of the first half of the century at least, farming and industrial labor were more intertwined.[17]

Even as many northeastern farm families were contributing to the creation of a manufacturing workforce, however, large numbers of others were pursuing versions of the republican ideal of rural independence by migrating westward to land seized or otherwise acquired from native Americans. For many settlers, this was a move away from the pressures and risks of market involvement. Moreover, historians in the Turnerian tradition have tended to see the acquisition of western land as a step towards economic equality, and the West as the source and guarantee of American democracy. The continued availability of western land left open the question of how far new U.S. regions would be drawn into markets for produce and labor. As in parts of the East, some pressures drew westerners into produce markets but others restrained their participation in wage labor.

The initial distribution of western lands was in fact far from equal. Although over time a growing proportion of newly available land was in government hands, much was controlled by land companies and other speculators whose subsequent distribution of it to purchasers and tenants created the material conditions under which western farming was established.[18] Except in the South and Southwest, where slavery permitted the extension of large-scale plantation farming, many parts of the West were divided into modest land holdings capable of development with family labor. Midwestern farm families continued to pursue strategies intended to secure independence and a living from the land for their children. But moving to, acquiring, and clearing new land commonly entailed costs and obligations that required a measure of cash-crop production to repay. Many New England farmers in New York or Ohio, for instance, established the kind of mixed-crop regimes they were used to back East, but added wheat as a field crop intended specifically for sale.[19] Obligations were familial and cultural as well as financial. Movement to the frontier often entailed a marked lowering of living standards already acquired at home. Continued cash-crop production, even alongside mixed farming for subsistence, was a way to earn the means for restoring through consumption material standards left behind. This desire was reinforced by evangelical notions of civility and respectability, and patterns of household consumption were also linked to the desire to create and maintain networks of sociability in a new environment. All these things led to a rising output of farm goods for shipment to southern, eastern, or international markets, for which manufactured goods were purchased in exchange.[20]

The absence of slavery ensured that much of the Midwest would develop a different set of relationships between farming, commerce, and investment than those evolving in the South. Whereas planters' direct control of land and slaves absorbed their ideological concerns and investment decisions, the lack of large amounts of dependent labor in the Midwest prevented the direct control of large farms and restrained the creation of an agrarian elite. Surpluses for investment were frequently put, not directly into farming itself, but into profiting from handling the goods that farmers sold and purchased. This "diversion" of capital from the land led to the creation and extension of a commercial system and transportation infrastructure that hastened the North's capitalist development. It also ensured, incidentally, that midwestern elites would be rooted largely in commerce, manufacture, and related activities, rather than in farming, giving them stronger affinities with their capitalist counterparts in the Northeast than with the slaveholding elites of the South.[21] These affinities would prove crucial to the political realignments that foreshadowed the Civil War.

The major regions of rural America therefore were characterized by commercial farming by the 1850s, but wage labor was not generally predominant in rural production. However, there were indications that this next step might be achieved. In some rural areas the essential characteristics of capitalism already had evolved within the system of agricultural production itself. Commercial farming based on the work of a rural proletariat was found in certain circumstances—in some wheat regions of the mid-Atlantic and Midwest, in market gardens near major cities, on the ranches and large farms being opened on the prairies and in California, and in the production of some specialist crops with heavy labor demands, such as the tobacco grown in the southern half of the Connecticut River Valley in New England. After an early period of general labor scarcity, farms in the Midwest also had come to provide employment for tens of thousands of hired laborers, some of them farmers' sons and emigrants from the East, an increasing number immigrants from Europe. Many facets of North America's initial high land-to-labor ratio were being reversed by the Civil War period. Conditions seemed ripe for a full-blown system of agrarian capitalism that would efface the regional distinctions that had helped give rise to it. By securing the abolition of slavery, the northern victory in the Civil War removed the most notable regional obstacle to its domination.

Yet agrarian capitalism was not fully established in the nineteenth century. Two of the most notable analysts of mid-nineteenth century agriculture have stressed its dual nature, as a way of life as well as a business; postwar events would tend to confirm this ambiguous character of American farming. Vast numbers of farmers continued to operate on a family and local-exchange basis. Many midwestern farmers would reduce their reliance on hired workers in the 1870s and 1880s. During and after Reconstruction, meanwhile, southern farming would evolve new forms of dependent labor in tenancy and sharecropping. To the extent that it would emerge even in the twentieth century, agrarian capitalism would require both massive capital investment and heavy government intervention to regulate markets and subsidize production.[22]

Before the twentieth century the role of the American countryside was less to create agrarian capitalism as such, than to contribute conditions in which commercial and industrial capitalism would flourish, especially in the Northeast and Upper Midwest. Whether by generating labor available for hire or diverting capital investment into commercial infrastructure, moderate-scaled, household-based farming in those regions helped create the circumstances for a profound economic and social transformation.

NOTES

1. On recent debates in rural history, see Allan Kulikoff, "The Transition to Capitalism in Rural America," *William and Mary Quarterly,* 46 (Jan. 1989), 120–44; Kulikoff, "Households and Markets: Towards a New Synthesis of American Agrarian History," *William and Mary Quarterly,* 50 (April

1993), 342–55; Christopher Clark, "Economics and Culture: Opening Up the Rural History of the Early American Northeast," *American Quarterly,* 43 (June 1991), 279–301; Michael Merrill, "Putting 'Capitalism' in its Place: A Review of Recent Literature," *William and Mary Quarterly,* 52 (April 1995), 315–26; Charles Post, "The Agrarian Origins of U.S. Capitalism: The Transformation of the Northern Countryside Before the Civil War," *Journal of Peasant Studies,* 22 (1995), 389–445. For full citations on the literature of the transition to capitalism, see note 4 in Paul A. Gilje, "The Rise of Capitalism," in this volume.

2. Christopher Clark, *The Roots of Rural Capitalism: Western Massachusetts, 1780–1860* (Ithaca, 1990), 15; see also Merrill, "Putting 'Capitalism' in its Place." On the emergence of wage labor, see Robert J. Steinfeld, *The Invention of Free Labor: The Employment Relation in English and American Law and Culture, 1350–1870* (Chapel Hill, 1991).

3. Daniel Vickers, "Competency and Competition: Economic Culture in Early America," *William and Mary Quarterly,* 47 (Jan. 1990), 3–29, suggests the interconnectedness of independent and market strategies in rural life; Charles G. Sellers, *The Market Revolution: Jacksonian America, 1815–1846* (New York, 1991), 3–33, suggests a more rigid opposition between "land" and "market." Susan Archer Mann, *Agrarian Capitalism in Theory and Practice* (Chapel Hill, 1990) discusses inherent obstacles to capitalist development in farming. On regional divisions, see W. Thomas Easterbrook, *North American Patterns of Growth and Development: The Continental Context* (Toronto, 1990).

4. See the essays in T. H. Aston and C. H. E. Philpin, eds., *The Brenner Debate: Agrarian Class Structure and Economic Development in Pre-Industrial Europe* (Cambridge, 1985).

5. Daniel Vickers, *Farmers and Fisherman: Two Centuries of Work in Essex County, Massachusetts, 1630–1830* (Chapel Hill, 1994); Allan Kulikoff, *The Agrarian Origins of American Capitalism* (Charlottesvile, 1992); Kulikoff, *Tobacco and Slaves: The Development of Southern Cultures in the Chesapeake, 1680–1800* (Chapel Hill, 1986); Gregory A. Stiverson, *Poverty in a Land of Plenty: Tenancy in Eighteenth-Century Maryland* (Baltimore, 1981).

6. Paul G. E. Clemens, *The Atlantic Economy and Colonial Maryland's Eastern Shore: From Tobacco to Grain* (Ithaca, 1980), chap. 6; Carville Earle, *Geographical Inquiry and American Historical Problems* (Stanford, 1992), 229.

7. Barry Levy, *Quakers and the American Family: British Settlement in the Delaware Valley* (New York, 1988), 14, 125, 152. Lucy Simler and Paul G. E. Clemens, "The 'Best Poor Man's Country' in 1783: The Population Structure of Rural Society in Late-Eighteenth-Century Southeastern Penn-

sylvania," *Proceedings of the American Philosophical Society*, 133 (June 1989), 243; Sharon V. Salinger, *'To Serve Well and Faithfully': Labor and Indentured Servants in Pennsylvania, 1682–1800* (Cambridge, 1987).

8. Kulikoff, *Agrarian Origins*, esp. chaps. 2 and 3; Kulikoff, "Households and Markets," 342–55. For a different emphasis, see Jeremy Atack and Fred Bateman, "Yeoman Farming: Antebellum America's Other 'Peculiar Institution,' " in Lou Ferleger, ed., *Agriculture and National Development: Views on the Nineteenth Century* (Ames, 1990), 25–51.

9. Vickers, *Farmers and Fisherman*, 206–19; Toby L. Ditz, *Property and Kinship: Inheritance in Early Connecticut, 1750–1820* (Princeton, 1986); Patricia Tracy, "Reconsidering Migration within Colonial New England," *Journal of Social History*, 23 (1989), 93–113; Kenneth L. Lockridge, "Land, Population and the Evolution of New England Society, 1630–1790," *Past and Present*, 39 (April 1968), 62–80.

10. Daniel M. Friedenberg, *Life, Liberty and the Pursuit of Land: The Plunder of Early America* (Buffalo, 1992); Andrew R. L. Cayton and Peter S. Onuf, *The Midwest and the Nation: Rethinking the History of an American Region* (Bloomington, 1990), 2–10; Alan Taylor, *William Cooper's Town: Power and Persuasion on the Frontier of the Early Republic* (New York, 1995).

11. Lee Soltow, *Distribution of Wealth and Income in the United States in 1798* (Pittsburgh, 1989).

12. Joseph P. Reidy, *From Slavery to Agrarian Capitalism in the Cotton Plantation South: Central Georgia, 1800–1880* (Chapel Hill, 1992), 14, 24, 30–32; Steven Hahn, *The Roots of Southern Populism: Yeoman Farmers and the Transformation of the Georgia Upcountry, 1850–1890* (New York, 1983); David F. Weiman, "Farmers and the Market in Antebellum America: A View from the Georgia Upcountry," *Journal of Economic History*, 47 (Sept. 1987) 627–47.

13. Peter Kolchin, *American Slavery, 1619–1877* (New York, 1993), 170–73; James Oakes, *Slavery and Freedom: An Interpretation of the Old South* (New York, 1990); Ira Berlin and Philip D. Morgan, eds., *Cultivation and Culture: Labor and the Shaping of Slave Life in the Americas* (Charlottesville, 1993); Charles C. Bolton, *Poor Whites of the Antebellum South: Tenants and Laborers in Central North Carolina and Northeast Mississippi* (Durham, 1994), 5; on the southern economy in general, see Fred Bateman and Thomas Weiss, *A Deplorable Scarcity: The Failure of Industrialization in the Slave Economy* (Chapel Hill, 1981); and Gavin Wright, *Old South, New South: Revolutions in the Southern Economy since the Civil War* (New York, 1986).

14. Carville Earle and Ronald Hoffman, "The Foundation of the Modern Economy: Agriculture and the Costs of Labor in the United States and England, 1800–1860," *American Historical Review*, 85 (1980), 1055–94;

Billy G. Smith, *The "Lower Sort": Philadelphia's Laboring People, 1750–1800* (Ithaca, 1990); Bruce Laurie, *The Working People of Philadelphia, 1800–1850* (Philadelphia, 1980).

15. Clark, *Roots of Rural Capitalism,* chaps. 3, 5, and 7; Jeanne Boydston, *Home and Work: Housework, Wages and the Ideology of Labor in the Early Republic* (New York, 1990); Jonathan Prude, *The Coming of Industrial Order: Town and Factory Life in Rural Massachusetts, 1831–1860* (Cambridge, 1983); Thomas Dublin, *Women at Work: The Transformation of Work and Community in Lowell, Massachusetts, 1826–1860* (New York, 1979).

16. For a New England–Mid-Atlantic comparison, see Adrienne D. Hood, "The Gender Division of Labor in the Production of Textiles in Eighteenth-Century Rural Pennsylvania (Rethinking the New England Model)," *Journal of Social History,* 27 (Spring 1994), 537–61; on dairying, see Joan M. Jensen, *Loosening the Bonds: Mid-Atlantic Farm Women, 1800–1850* (New Haven, 1986); and Sally McMurry, *Transforming Rural Life: Dairying Families and Agricultural Change, 1820–1885* (Baltimore, 1995).

17. Thomas Dublin, *Transforming Women's Work: New England Lives in the Industrial Revolution* (Ithaca, 1994), chaps. 2 and 4; Hood, "The Gender Division of Labor." See also Mary Blewett, *Men, Women, and Work: Class, Gender and Protest in the New England Shoe Industry, 1790–1910* (Urbana, 1988).

18. On land distribution see, for example, W. Eugene Harper, *The Transformation of Western Pennsylvania, 1770–1800* (Pittsburgh, 1991), chap. 2; and Soltow, *Distribution of Wealth and Income,* 68–69, 79.

19. Cayton and Onuf, *The Midwest and the Nation,* 30–44, and John Mack Faragher, *Sugar Creek: Life on the Illinois Prairie* (New Haven, 1986) note the continued pursuit of household independence by western farmers and the use of markets to this end. On wheat, see Robert Leslie Jones, *History of Agriculture in Ohio to 1880* (Kent, 1983), 59.

20. Lori Merish, "'The Hand of Refined Taste' in the Frontier Landscape: Caroline Kirkland's *A New Home, Who'll Follow?* and the Feminization of American Consumerism," *American Quarterly,* 45 (Dec. 1993), 485–523; on sociability, see Karen V. Hansen, *A Very Social Time: Crafting Community in Antebellum New England* (Berkeley, 1994), esp. chap. 4; on farm consumption see Sally McMurry, *Families and Farmhouses in Nineteenth Century America: Vernacular Design and Social Change* (New York, 1988), 135–69.

21. On commercial developments based on agricultural produce, see William Cronon, *Nature's Metropolis: Chicago and the Great West* (New York, 1991); and Timothy R. Mahoney, *River Towns in the Great West: the Structure of Provincial Urbanization in the American Midwest, 1820–1870* (Cambridge, 1990). Joseph F. Rishel, *Founding Families of Pittsburgh: The Evolu-*

tion of a Regional Elite, 1760–1910 (Pittsburgh, 1990), 82, notes the declining proportion of people with farming backgrounds in urban elite composition.

22. Jeremy Atack and Fred Bateman, *To their Own Soil: Agriculture in the Antebellum North* (Ames, 1987). Mann, *Agrarian Capitalism in Theory and Practice*. On the Midwest, see also Harriet Friedmann, "World-Market, State and Family Farm: Social Bases of Household Production in the Era of Wage Labor," *Comparative Studies in Society and History*, 20 (Oct. 1978), 545–86. On the South, see Roger L. Ransom and Richard Sutch, *One Kind of Freedom: The Economic Consequences of Emancipation* (Cambridge, 1977); and Wright, *Old South, New South.*

FIVE

Capitalism, Industrialization, and the Factory in Post-revolutionary America

JONATHAN PRUDE

THE EARLY AMERICAN FACTORY SEEMS SELF-EVIDENT. Through count-less pronouncements, conventional wisdom has made this institu-tion a central emblem of pivotal economic changes transforming the republic—and the northern tier of the republic particularly—between the Revolution and the Civil War. Mention industrializa-tion in this period and think of factories growing steadily more plentiful. Nor is it just any kind of factory that comes to mind. Exemplified preeminently by visions of New England and Middle Atlantic textile mills, the notion of factory commonly associated with this era conforms to a fixed stereotype. Say factory in these years and think less of assorted possibilities than of a singular phenomenon: big and solid buildings; edifices filled with large numbers of workers, many of them of limited skill and often fe-male; and structures brimming most notably with power-driven production technologies. Say early American factories and think of large scale manufacturing bolstered by machines. Think of waterwheels and here and there of smokestacks. What else is there to know?

In some sense perhaps not too much. Certainly there is com-pelling convenience in focusing upon this version of the early factory, for represented this way the organization of factory production yields a convenient shortcut to understanding the complex shifts encompassed by postrevolutionary industrialization. See factories and comprehend many of the changes overtaking antebellum manufacturing. Aside from such heuristic service, moreover, the concrete role of hefty mechanized workplaces—with cotton and woolen mills leading the way—was in itself indisputably significant. And a good portion of the essay that follows will thus inevitably draw on the story of these enterprises.

Yet, from another perspective, simply keying to the stereotype is scarcely sufficient. For one thing, invoking the early factory's familiar representation does not address the vitally important issues of how and why this kind of manufacturing arose in the republic, and of the ramifying consequences it unleashed. Moreover, even before taking up these fundamental topics, there is reason to go beyond the stereotype. Specifically, there is reason to begin our discussion by stepping back and examining what, at its most basic level, the early factory really was. And following on from this examination, there is reason to consider the twinned possibilities that the factory, whatever it was, did not provide the only vehicle for antebellum industrialization and yet, at the same time, that the factory, given what it ultimately was, cast substantial influence over the economy, in part because it could assume a number of different forms. There is reason, in sum, to begin by taking a wider and more contextually alert view of this institution. For only with this as our starting point will we be able to gauge precisely how the early factory participated in the recastings of manufacturing arising in the young nation.

WHAT, THEN, WAS THE EARLY FACTORY? Well into the nineteenth century, the word "factory" carried two meanings. There was, first, a definition dating from the fifteenth century that specified the term as an establishment where traders (or "factors") conducted business. A second meaning, surfacing in the seventeenth century, deployed "factory" as a contraction of manufactory or workshop, a place where something was made. This latter meaning soon grew dominant. But it merits emphasis that while everyday parlance was likely associating factories with water-powered textile mills by the early 1800s, there was no formal lexographical connection in the antebellum era between factory and mill, or between factory and sizable mechanized workplaces of any kind. Insofar as factory meant manufactory, it was a term contemporaries could properly apply to various arenas of production.[1]

The gap between this record of relaxed pre-Civil War usage and the more precise connotations commonly attached to factories today is plainly substantial. And although this is not the place to delve into exactly when the narrowed modern connotation gained currency, the contribution recent historians have made to the process does bear notice. Because scholars have in truth played a salient role. Indeed, those of us who at one point or another since the 1970s have written about the antebellum textile industry may have done our share by willy-nilly advancing the impression that the mills we studied were the factories *par excellence* of their time. But probably more consequential in this regard have been the historians whose research has dealt with a range of non-agricultural work situations. The resulting inventories of manufacturing venues—especially those advanced by students of urban industrialization like Bruce Laurie and Sean Wilentz—typically distinguish between a small array of large, elaborately organized, and above all mechanized "factories" (filled with largely unskilled laborers) on the one hand, and a far more numerous assortment of less ample and mechanically more innocent workplaces on the other. Hence under this second heading we discover multitudes of: "manufactories" (hosting upwards of 20 or 25 hands); more modest sweatshops and garrets; artisan shops; and the often home-based work sites of outworkers.[2]

Scholars have thus in effect tended to adopt the stereotyped rendering of factories: factories as big and machine-equipped. Yet they have characteristically done so less to highlight the influence of such establishments than to minimize their presence in the economic landscape. If the factory they typically conjure up resembles the enterprise of conventional wisdom, it shares little of the panache conventional wisdom usually assigns to factories. Factories by many scholarly reckonings turned out yarn and cloth; they also included some of the foundries, armories, and printing enterprises of the period. But factories by this same estimate had little to do (for example) with the unmechanized outpouring of shoes and garments, two major sectors of early nineteenth-century manufacturing. So that far from standing as an icon for a new economic order, the factory enshrined in much of current historiography played only a modest part in the drama of antebellum economic change.[3]

Now this interpretive angle has much to recommend it. If nothing else, it underscores the heterogeneity that surely conditioned the transformation of pre-Civil War nonagricultural production. But there are also problems with this approach. For one thing, an analytic framework centering concertedly on large size and the presence of skill-eroding machines tends to downplay the myriad possibilities encompassed even among factories narrowly construed—even among textile mills. After all, concentrating on fixed definitional criteria makes it hard to remember that antebellum mills ranged from genuinely large "Lowell"-style plants situated in northeastern urban or urbanizing locales, to scores of comparatively smaller "country" mills rooted in northern rural communities, to metropolitan mills that sprang up in settings like Philadelphia and that themselves extended from major free-standing structures to single floors of buildings, and on finally to the sprinklings of mills that took hold in the South—some of them recruiting slave laborers and all of them demonstrating that the concentration of antebellum industrial manufacture in the North did not totally preclude textile factories below the Mason-Dixon Line.[4]

But besides obscuring the mixture of forms attaching even to strictly conceptualized factories, cleaving to rigid specifications can present another difficulty. It can cause us to overstate the line between factory and nonfactory styles of manufacturing, turning an awareness of the many guises of industrialization into a misleadingly reified threshold that ignores both the back and forth hybridization often occurring between these categories and the presence of enterprises that performed like factories even while bearing little resemblance to textile mills. Seizing upon fixed standards, in sum, can cause us to misrepresent fundamentally the role of factories within the industrializing process. For although it may well make sense to concede factories were not as universal as early nineteenth century definitions imply and were less robustly influential than conventional wisdom indicates, it may well also make sense to insist they were more broadly diverse and significant than historians have come to assume.

To pursue this latter line of argument, however, requires another review of terms. What, after all, do we mean by "industrialization" in this period? Most writers on America regard industrialization as closely linked to advances in capitalism. But then what was "capitalism" in this context? The origins and initial character of capitalism on this side of the Atlantic (and above all in the rural Northeast) has of course been a vexed topic among historians in recent years. But by way of offering a few baseline propositions, it seems reasonable to posit colonial and provincial America as a milieu in which social and economic patterns that centered on limited market structures, on strategies of communal and household cooperation, and on nonprofit priorities coexisted with a systemic commitment to private property, with swatches of staple husbandry and wage labor, and with clottings of emphatically profit-geared mercantile activity and land speculation.

Such a milieu was demonstrably not without capitalistic elements; and it would not necessarily have evolved into more full-blown capitalism in ways as seismically wrenching as those the Old World experienced in passing into capitalism from its antecedent array of feudalistic and premodern modes of exchange and production. Yet it is equally plausible to propose that America, whatever its colonial precursors to subsequent economic development, exhibited a qualitatively augmented embrace of capitalism during the years of young nationhood. This quickening postrevolutionary metamorphosis involved a substantially deepened dependence on market relations, particularly relations attending nonlocal commercial exchanges. It also involved a qualitatively sharpened focus on profit as the guiding goal of economic transactions. And it involved for the most part notable increments in free wage labor and in the ranks of individuals who stood to such labor not as masters or patrons but as supervisors, employers, or capitalist investors.[5]

The deepened post-1789 grip of capitalist activity was by no means universal. While the South evinced growth and structural change (witness the presence of southern textile mills), the south-ern economy as a whole retained a distinctive trajectory (as shown by its sustained reliance on chattel labor, even inside textile facto-ries, and its comparatively slow engagement with new commercial and other industrial ventures).[6] And while the North, for its part, emerged as the region hosting the most vigorous postrevolutionary strides into capitalism, it too revealed hesitations. There were ample instances of northerners evincing outlooks—often grounded in tra-ditional notions of community, household, and craft-based commonweal—quite at odds with the thrust of new developments. The novel patterns of capitalist change were consequently often surrounded and deeply conditioned by quite different orientations. Still, especially in the North, the broadly reverberating pressures and consequences of capitalist change penetrated both cities and the countryside.

"Industrialization" as it transpired in the early republic was an element of this mounting curve of change. Again arising most pronouncedly in the North, industrialization is best understood as a form of manufacturing generating expanded volumes of cheap goods intended for sale through extensive market networks. De-riving at times from domestic manufacturing (under which house-hold members had forged items for their own use), but often build-ing upon, and supplanting, craft manufacturing (under which artisans toiling alongside journeymen and apprentices fashioned products in their entirety and sold them principally to local cus-tomers), industrialization in this period was in some cases unques-tionably aided by technology. But as part of the pronounced vari-ability of postrevolutionary economic change, early industrialization could as easily proceed without machines as with them. What in-dustrialization in this era ultimately required—what was ultimately its distinguishing feature—was a decisive increment in division of labor. America's early industrial revolution rested above all on the ability of manufacturers to increase output and decrease unit costs by carving up production into smaller tasks.

And factories? Factories were venues of centralized industrial-ization. As a further sign of its innate heterogeneity, early industri-alization not only embraced both mechanized and unmechanized work operations, it also enfolded markedly different configurations of laborers. The division of labor it rested upon could be accomplished by doling out subsidiary processes to networks of employees in decentralized workplaces, including the workers' own homes, situated alike in urban neighborhoods and hinterland communities. Or it could entail gathering workers together in centralized work spaces. Or it might involve both centralized and decentralized arrangements. Segments of the early Northern textile industry, for example, were well known for combining the production of yarn in mills with the manufacture of cloth by outworking handloom weavers, many of them rural women laboring at home. But the point in any case is that the tilt toward blending divisions of labor with some measure of centralization was embodied in factories.

Early factories, in sum, were about organization as much as the length of work rosters or the roar of intricate machines. They were not a thing so much as a spectrum of things, and in some respects not only a spectrum of things but an ongoing process—the principal of centralization. There is thus no reason not to lower the minimal size of factories to fifteen or even ten workers. And if we do this as well as relax the technology requirement, we can begin to conceive of factories as extending not only through all kinds of plants spitting out yarn and cloth but also to at least portions of the manufactories, sweatshops, and garrets that were so important to northern industrialization. In its turn, of course, enhancing the scope of our subject in this manner inevitably highlights and clarifies how the supposedly clearcut demarcation of factory versus nonfactory often in practice was crossed and recrossed. Thus we see that supposedly sub-factory workplaces (like certain small paper mills) were mechanized while irreproachably large and mechanized enterprises (such as various armories) in fact supported contingents of highly skilled artisans. And finally, overall, reaching for this more capacious understanding permits us to appreciate how deeply factories were embedded in the sweep of early industrialization. Certainly, for example, positing these enterprises as both large and small, as both machined and machineless, alerts us to the frequency with which factories were synchronized with other, more dispersed formats of production. For it turns out that the combination of outwork and concentrated labor that subsisted in the textile industry also arose elsewhere in the economy. Indeed, it played out even in shoe and clothing manufacture where "putting out" soon enough coincided with "central shops" from which materials were dispatched but in which (even before the introduction of sewing machines and their female attendants in the 1850s) teams of cloth cutters and shoe workers took up stations. As in textiles, so in footwear and garments, early American industrialization joined factories and nonfactories at the hip.[7]

My aim in advancing this view is not to make definitional calibrations the subject under review. Still less is it my intention to so broaden the meaning of factory that what is meant fades into a blur. Factories construed as centralized industrialization—or for that matter as continuing processes of centralization—still stood out from abiding artisinal shops with their appreciably less divided labor; and whatever their bonds to outwork, factories were likewise still distinguishable from the plentiful instances of decentralized production. Rather, my purpose is to cast early factories in proper proportion and so illuminate how they did in fact fit within the economic retoolings of the new republic.

BUT WHAT OF THE OTHER SUBSTANTIVE issues raised at the outset. What, for instance, was the genesis of the factory? Where did it come from? Scattered versions of sizable workplaces with at least hints of division of labor can be found in the eighteenth century. (If nowhere else, they appear in the form of the notoriously shortlived cloth manufactories that doubled as poor relief by assigning the down and out to toil at spinning wheels and handlooms).[8] A more trenchant emergence of factories, however, took place amidst the postrevolutionary push (most notably in the North) to augment manufacturing output. And this shift, expressed as often as not in movements toward industrial manufacture, reflected complex entanglements with demand. While evolving differently in different economic sectors, self-reinforcing circuits of demand and production took shape after 1789, ensuring that a growing desire for goods called forth increased manufacturing capacity, which then further stimulated demand. Facilitated by new governmental policies and credit arrangements, and critically bolstered by legions of western and southern customers hungry for cheap versions of consumer goods like cloth, clothing, and shoes, industrialization—including its factory variant—grew apace in response to a far-flung market that was itself continually nurtured by the availability of products.

The specific shifts in manufacturing which thus ensued could take place incrementally, almost seamlessly. In the northern countryside, for example, there was rarely any immediate sense of rupture when rural women slipped into the ranks of paid outworkers serving networks of industrial production. Many of these outworkers (like those weaving cloth for early spinning mills) were simply applying skills familiar to farming wives and daughters. And the goal initially drawing these women into their new employments lay less in profit-centered desire to maximize their family's incomes than in the less disruptive (and less robustly capitalistic) wish merely to keep household economy afloat.[9]

Even the move to centralize production could at first seem conventional and commonplace. The modest requirements associated with setting up smaller versions of machineless factories (by clothing subcontractors, say) permitted these workplaces to sprout with little fanfare. Machine-filled factories naturally necessitated bigger efforts. Leaving aside the vast capital raised by leading Yankee merchants to finance the huge Lowell-style mills, early country textile factories required anywhere from $10,000 to $40,000 to get started; in 1855, paper mills in Berkshire County, Massachusetts needed almost $30,000.[10] These were substantial sums. Yet they were not so great that investing in the smaller renditions of woolen, cotton, and paper factories seemed an unreasonable or unexpected tactic for congeries of moderately wealthy (rather than exceptionally rich) farmers, tradesmen, and storekeeper-merchants. What is more, the very buildings constituting the first wave of textile and paper factories tended to look familiar, bearing the appearance of barns or churches more than of some shrill architectural declarations of novelty.

But this vision of smooth and unreflected change has limits. Precisely because postrevolutionary capitalism constantly bumped against alternative attitudes and structures, the transformations in manufacturing after 1789 could cause disorientation and concern, with even changes originally experienced as benign ultimately coming to seem decidedly problematic. (It is not too much to suggest, in fact, that along with division of labor, the often-conflicted

confluence of new and old was the talismatic core of industrialization in this era.) Thus, the northern hinterland women who shoul-
dered industrial outwork to preserve their household status-quo
might in the end worriedly realize first, that the cash incomes they
needed to retain economic equilibrium actually signalled an accel-
erating dependency on the market, and second, that outwork left
them increasingly answerable to the intrusive authority of extra-
domestic employers. But concern arose, too, over the specific introduction of centralized manufactories. Farmers worried about
losing labor to factories, and in the case of textile mills they worried about the threat mill dams posed to customary access to local
streams.[11] And then, of course, there were artisans—in both cities
and the hinterland—who at various junctures, and with varying
levels of urgency, bridled at the competition brought by industrial
production and its crystallization in factories.

If it is important to avoid presenting early industrialization as
an untroubled segue from what came before, it is equally important to avoid describing the process as somehow automatic. To
stress that many industrial ventures—not excepting factories—were
physically and financially unimposing does not mean these ventures were any less a function of concrete decisions. Nor does not-
ing that industrialization took shape in response to broad dialec-
tics of demand and output preclude emphasizing that the
entrepreneurs most directly responsible for launching these industrial enterprises, and particularly the individuals assuming
significant proprietary roles, did so for their own clear-eyed purpose: gain. As stridently as anyone in the early republic, these figures
(to appropriate a contemporary squib on one of them) turned their
energies to "deep calculations and [their] calculations [were of]
wealth."[12]

To be sure, this ethos was not so much unprecedented as
unprecedentedly empowered to take hold and have consequence
in America's national economic environment. And even in this period, there was naturally a spectrum of ambitions. The expectations of a wealthy country mill master like Samuel Slater or the
eminent business families directing Lowell were of a different order from the expectations driving proprietors and managers of
most smaller textile operations—and both these outlooks differed
from the expectations animating the hustling small bosses of many

shoe and garment shops. (It is worth recalling in this context that in the early stages of industrial growth some manufacturing entrepreneurs willingly joined with craftsmen and farmers in supporting Democratic-Republicans against the aggressively capitalist agenda of the Federalist mercantile elite.) Nonetheless, if a firmer orientation to profit helped mark postrevolutionary capitalism, then the quest for accumulation surely looms as a particular causal motivation behind particular industrial projects. In fact, as recent research has demonstrated, even the introduction of machines into factory settings is best interpreted not as a metahistorical consequence of technological "efficiency" but as the thoroughly historical result of entrepreneurs guessing—ironically often on the basis of questionable data—that certain machines might yield acceptable returns.[13] None of this is surprising, for it amounts to saying only that the engineers of capitalist growth drew sustenance from capitalist dreams. Yet to say as much may remind us that amidst the countervailing pulls of eagerness for change and ambivalence over what change brought, the coming of industrial order—and of factories—happened because specific people acted for specific reasons.

THE CREATION OF FACTORIES DID NOT guarantee their survival. The contingency implicit in the human agency behind the formation of these institutions continued past their origins. And this, along with impressive failure rates among early industrial ventures of all kinds, meant it was some time before antebellum Americans were persuaded that industrialization, and centralized industrial manufacturing specifically, had long term prospects in their land. Still, by the 1830s and 1840s (and probably earlier in the case of textile mills) it seemed broadly evident that factories would not soon vanish. Which raises the problem of consequences: what difference did early factories make, especially to the northern states they primarily inhabited?

Increased output is one obvious answer. But since I have already evoked expanded productivity as a defining aspect of factories, let us turn to other consequences. Let us consider, to start with, their cultural ripplings. At least some portion of these enterprises acquired the emblematic weight of standing for the whole process of economic transformation. Led by armories and (especially) textile mills, larger mechanized factories of the era became lighting rods in the formal discourse over change in the republic. Should America industrialize? If so, need it (God forbid!) follow Britain's putatively degraded example of "satanic mills" and impoverished laborers or could it find more pleasant routes into modernity? Such queries in books, pamphlets, and speeches, not infrequently found voice through debates over factories—which in this sense actually did resemble the icon of industrialization set forth by modern conventional wisdom.[14]

But the impact of early factories upon the period's cultural politics was complex. If structures of centralized manufacturing exemplified a new order, they also mystified it. As a pronounced expression of the drift of labor from home to workplace, factories placed employees in enclosed settings not readily accessible to outsiders. Reformers, journalists, and even tourists might visit such venues, just as they peered "sympathetically" into settings of antebellum poverty. Such observations, however, were sporadic. And while glimpses into factories might yield the occasional glowing report, they were as prone as any descent into slums to carry the flavor of venturing into exotic terrains. By the same token, fiction proved slow to venture inside factories. And "better" paintings of the period (especially "genre" canvases) tended either to avoid industrialization or to offer distant exterior views of factories (usually mills) tucked into the comfortable middle distance of rural landscapes: a trope doubtless intended to soothe anxieties about factories but one that could not help contributing to brooding cultural uncertainties over what transpired within their walls.

On the other hand, postrevolutionary factories registered the opposite of mystery, for they were among the most rigorously monitored work settings of their time. Admittedly, other contemporary undertakings (including larger southern plantations) adopted at least the form of tight labor regimens. But the exigencies of coordinating centralized division of labor and, when technologies were involved, of enforcing the discipline of smooth machine-production—all this encouraged an intensified managerial control. (Indeed, factory-style management could even touch outworkers connected to factories, as when outlying garment makers were obliged to bring their work to employers for inspection, or more blatantly when factory proprietors drew outworkers into central workplaces expressly to impose greater control over them.[15]) Despite gentling gestures of paternalism and intervening tiers of "inside contracting" within some establishments, early factories were cathedrals of concentrated hierarchical supervision.[16] Extending (in many instances) from owners through bureaucratic "rules and regulations" and resident agents and finally down to room "overlookers," the administration of factories demonstrated sharply calibrated lines of top-down authority. Especially in the North, and especially when set against the republic's supposed commitment to democratic political governance, this structure of influence could itself raise further concern over industrialization. But it assuredly also signified the means by which the opaqueness of centralized industrial work was balanced by efforts to regulate laborers precisely by bringing them under close observation.

And what of the laborers thus observed? What consequences did factories hold for their employees? Once again the answer is complex. For some working people, or for some of them some of the time, industrialization and factories held important leavening implications. Because it was frequently open to females, industrial employment proffered new occupational possibilities to women and girls; and for this constituency the conjunction of wages and the exiting from home that often accompanied factory employment (most famously premarital employment in mills) could nurture new confidence and self-awareness. There were, besides, laboring folk for whom factories spelled outright economic relief: hardpressed hinterland families who signed on as household units in country mills; or foreign immigrants who scrambled into all available industrial employment, including factory slots; or transplanted rural sorts who secured jobs in urban manufacturing, again including centralized workshops. In fact, even artisans, for all their resentment of deskilled production, could benefit. More than a few master craftsmen turned into the entrepreneurs orchestrating industrialization. Others landed jobs among the emerging corps of factory supervisors or amid the skilled positions which (as suggested earlier) subsisted in some factories. All things considered, it was probably quite rare for full-fledged artisans personally to undergo demotion into unskilled or semiskilled factory jobs. And the low capitalization costs of smaller factories may have aided lesser craftsmen and journeymen in attaining the dignity of proprietorship.[17]

But the other side of the balance sheet is no less compelling. To start with, the willingness of northern industrial enterprises to hire women, families, and newcomers did not extend to African Americans. The region's industrial laborforce, and its factory laborforce above all, was cast firmly in whiteface, with the result that northern blacks were unable to participate in a significant sphere of paying work. Yet the workers who were hired did not necessarily find their situation benign. Certainly, to follow one fault line of industrial employment, the disturbance stemming from extra-domestic authority imposed on families through outwork weighed far more heavily when workers entered factories. For in practice country mills were known to intrude between parents and children on their payrolls, while mill girls not infrequently discovered painful dissidence between their roles as gainfully employed operatives and their identities as females in a society still imbued with patriarchy.[18]

Nor were the financial rewards of factory stints uniformly attractive. Taken as a whole, industrialization expressed and exacerbated widening gaps in income distribution, and its most "sweated" spheres (in the non-factory outworker sectors of the clothing trade) held appalling conditions. Wages in larger mechanized factories generally stood at the higher end of industrial pay scales, both for whatever skilled laborers they used and for machine tenders (though the latter mostly female operatives always earned less than the former invariably male employees). But smaller factories paid less well; and over time even managers of textile mills responded to mounting competition by maintaining long hours and restricting wage hikes below rises in productivity.[19] As a result, factory work may have permitted some laborers to purchase some of the goods industrialization was turning out and needed to have purchased. By the same token, however, the income awarded to the bulk of less skilled workers nitched into through factory berths left wide seams of the industrial laborforce struggling to purchase the necessities of life, not excluding the manufactured items upon which they now increasingly depended.

Combined with the regimen of watchful discipline conditioning early factories, these tensions and constraints helped define the industrial order and turned factories into unsettled amalgams of opportunity and wearisome pressure. How—to raise the final consequence we will consider—did factory workers respond to this mix? How did they react to what they experienced?[20] It is entirely possible to show that industrial laborers as a group more or less accepted all that befell them. Put concretely, it is possible to marshal evidence that such workers did not demonstrate permanent overarching organizational unity, decisive political interventions, or the capacity to launch strikes that were more than episodically successful. And it is possible to demonstrate that industrial workers in centralized workplaces were particularly cut off from effective resistance, their assertiveness vitiated (in the case of mill hands, for example) by their tendency to linger only briefly in given work sites, by the special difficulty women operatives faced in turning defiant, and (especially after 1850 and the infusion of foreign workers) by ethnic fissures.

To leave matters there, however, would be patently misleading. If early industrial workers did not all join militantly together inside a single long-lasting institutional framework of labor militancy, it is no less true that numerous labor and labor-supporting organizations flowered in these years. Ranging from trade unions and alliances constructed on the fundaments of craft heritage all the way to clubs and "societies" rooted in neighborhoods or reformist programs, these organizations provided intermittent yet appreciable links among laborers in industrializing situations. Moreover, such structured connections, issued at least occasionally into explicit political activities; and the trade-oriented liaisons fostered "turnouts" which, whatever their spotty efficacy, were frequent enough to disclose the strength of labor disquiet brewing in the antebellum North. Just as consequentially, these linkages comprised institutional spaces for industrial laboring people to preserve plebeian traditions and transmute "middle-class" norms into their own codes of values and behavior—in other words to maintain and create elements of a working-class culture. And factory workers, even female factory workers, were part of all this. Thus women mill operatives assembled several organizations, enjoyed at least occasional and loose contact with other laborers' associations, and participated in petition campaigns to state legislators. Thus, too, residents of New England mill villages, assuredly including women, used bonds sparked by evangelical revivals to enact some of the most vigorous assertions of plebeian values to unfold in the pre-Civil War North. And finally, although textile employees were comparatively less enthusiastic about strikes than other industrial laborers, textile hands—with mill girls again prominent among them—mounted their share of turnouts. So also female shoeworkers (who had initiated job actions even as outworkers) played a crucial role in the great shoe strike of 1860.[21]

Such restiveness did not happen all at once. There were rhythms shaping the efforts of workers to push back, surges and diminuendoes in militancy according to the conditions laborers faced. What is more, some industrial employees may also have experienced what amounted to a turning point. Like other Americans, early factory operatives had to be persuaded that centralized industrial establishments were not a passing fancy. And there are signs that when certain of these laborers were so persuaded, their resistance shifted ground, becoming on balance less focused on dismissing factories *tout court* and more on learning how to play the game of factory employment. Among these workers, portions of the structured responses just described—the forging of organizations and political actions, the strikes and cultural formations—represented exactly this latter kind of coping with ongoing factories. Hence, for these laborers, there were components of plebeian structured reactions that came only *after* factories were in some degree accepted. Which in turn suggests there were operatives for whom these same orchestrated reactions arose on the other side of a transition from prior, more rejectionist orientations: orientations that had previously given heavy play to simply quitting factory toil and also, now and again, to efforts (or rumors of efforts) aimed at outright destruction of concentrated industrial facilities.[22]

But there is also the suggestion here that even when workers had accepted that factories would probably persevere, resistance went beyond the structured forms we have denoted. Learning the factory game was a multifaceted exercise that often meant discrete as well as explicit and overt maneuverings. It meant that workers interrupted daily routines not just by turning out but also by covertly and individually stopping machines (to give themselves temporary respites) or by stealing material (to award themselves informal wage supplements.) It meant that inasmuch as laborers grew increasingly enmeshed in factory work (so that an employment record of brief stints might actually involve years of moving among factory berths), there emerged cohorts of operatives who took advantage of tight labor markets by using the possibility of switching jobs as a softly voiced yet crucial bargaining chip with their employers. It meant that workers, displaying remarkable energy and ingenuity, confronted the novelty of factory conditions—the inescapable divisions of industrial labor, the discipline and supervision, and sometimes the "perpetual" machines—by unilaterally constructing standards of "acceptable" factory work. Though collective, this last strategy was nonetheless at least initially another essentially undercover procedure, surfacing as directly confrontational only when the standards thus formulated were judged by workers to have been violated by managerial decisions to boost work loads or cut pay. And the sources bear hints of still more tacit gestures: the use of conspicuous consumption to signify wage earning autonomy, for example. But what has been said is perhaps sufficient to indicate that such quiet strategies may actually have been where factory workers invested their greatest energy. Workers under especially tight regimens may have been especially given to pressing their interests sotto voce. Indeed, it may be that the capacity of factory workers to formulate these strategies constituted their special contribution to both the strength and subtle texture of class configurations in antebellum America.[23]

THE EARLY FACTORY IS MANIFESTLY NOT all there is to say about early industrialization. Braided into the heterogeneous alterations of manufacturing occurring in this period (and hence into the variegated moltings of postrevolutionary capitalism), factories were only part of what happened in these years. Nor were they irreplaceable. If early nineteenth-century patterns revealed factories as more than momentary experiments, subsequent economic "progress" encompassed the counter-growth of decentralized industrialization in some sectors and even (in recent times) the explosive rise of neo-cottage industries. Yet the early factory did have particular and considerable influence on life and work in post-1789 America. If we are careful, if we pay mind both to the meaning of the terms we use and to what else was going on, we would do well to think long and hard about the factory in the early republic.

NOTES

1. *Oxford English Dictionary* (1888; 2nd ed., Oxford, Eng., 1989); *Compendious Dictionary of the English Language . . .* by Noah Webster (New Haven, 1806); *An American Dictionary of the English Language . . .* by Noah Webster (New York, 1835); *An American Dictionary of the English Language . . .* by Noah Webster (Springfield, MA, 1858). See also Mitford M. Mathews, *A Dictionary of Americanisms on Historical Principles* (Chicago, 1951).

2. Bruce Laurie, *Working People of Philadelphia, 1800–1850* (Philadelphia, 1980), 15–26; Sean Wilentz, *Chants Democratic: New York City & the Rise of the American Working Class, 1788–1850* (New York, 1984), 113–15. See also the roughly comparable set of divisions—"home, shop, factory"—proposed by Richard B. Stott in *Workers in the Metropolis: Class, Ethnicity, and Youth in Antebellum New York City* (Ithaca, 1990), 123–27.

3. On iron-making and printing, see Laurie, *Working People of Philadelphia*, 15; Wilentz, *Chants Democratic*, 114; Stott, *Workers in the Metropolis*, 43–46, 49–52; and Merritt Roe Smith, *Harpers Ferry Armory and the New Technology: The Challenge of Change* (Ithaca, 1977). On shoemaking and clothing manufacturing, see Mary H. Blewett, *Men, Women, and Work: Class, Gender, and Protest in the New England Shoe Industry, 1780– 1910* (Urbana, 1990), chaps. 1–5; Wilentz, *Chants Democratic*, 119–27; and Stott, *Workers in the Metropolis*, 37–42.

4. On the antebellum textile industry, see generally Caroline F. Ware, *The Early New England Cotton Manufacture: A Study in Industrial Beginnings* (Boston, 1931); Thomas Dublin, *Women at Work: The Transformation of Work and Community in Lowell, Massachusetts, 1826–1860* (New York, 1979); Jonathan Prude, *The Coming of Industrial Order: Town and Factory Life in Rural Massachusetts, 1810–1860* (Cambridge, 1983); Philip Scranton, *Proprietary Capitalism: The Textile Manufacture at Philadelphia, 1800–1885* (Cambridge, 1983); and Robert S. Starobin, *Industrial Slavery in the Old South* (New York, 1970), 12–14.

5. Cited in note 4 in Paul A. Gilje, "The Rise of Capitalism," in this volume.

6. See generally Peter Kolchin, *American Slavery, 1619–1877* (New York, 1993), 174–79.

7. On the role of outworkers in early industrialization, see generally Christopher Clark, *The Roots of Rural Capitalism: Western Massachusetts,*

1780–1860 (Ithaca, 1990), esp. chap. 5; Thomas Dublin, *Transforming Women's Work: New England Lives in the Industrial Revolution* (Ithaca, 1994), chap. 2; Prude, *Coming of Industrial Order*, 72–78; and Blewett, *Men, Women, and Work*, chaps. 2–3. On the role of "central shops," see Blewett, *Men, Women, and Work*, 22, 73, 97–99, 101–03; and Wilentz, *Chants Democratic*, 121–22. For the entry of machine tending women into central shops, see Egal Feldman, *Fit For Men: A Study of New York's Clothing Trade* (Washington, DC, 1960), 98–99.

8. Gary B. Nash, *The Urban Crucible: Social Change, Political Consciousness, and the Origins of the American Revolution* (Cambridge, MA, 1979), 189–96, 254–55, 327–38.

9. Prude, *Coming of Industrial Order*, 77; Christopher Clark, "Household Economy, Market Exchange and the Rise of Capitalism in the Connecticut Valley, 1800–1860," *Journal of Social History*, 13 (Winter 1979), 178, 180.

10. Wilentz, *Chants Democratic*, 116–17. Dublin, *Women at Work*, 17, 19; Peter J. Coleman, *The Transformation of Rhode Island, 1790–1860* (Providence, 1963), 93, 98; Judith A. McGaw, *Most Wonderful Machine: Mechanization and Social Change in Berkshire Paper Making, 1801–1885* (Princeton, 1987), 133.

11. Clark, "Household Economy," 180–81, 183. Gary Kulik, "Dams, Fish, and Farmers: Defense of Public Rights in Eighteenth–Century Rhode Island," in Steven Hahn and Jonathan Prude, eds., *The Countryside in the Age of Capitalist Transformation: Essays in the Social History of Rural America* (Chapel Hill, 1985), 25–50.

12. The quote is from an homage to Samuel Slater printed in the Pawtucket (RI) *Chronicle*, May 1, 1835.

13. McGaw, *Most Wonderful Machine*, chaps. 4–6. For an influential argument that early industrial production was organized less to promote pure economic efficiency than to ensure profit to nonworkers, see Stephen A. Marglin, "What Do Bosses Do? The Origins and Functions of Hierarchy in Capitalist Production," *The Review of Radical Political Economics*, 6 (Spring 1974), 60–112.

14. Thus the frequent invitation by proponents of industrialization to use the textile mill as a model for prescribed rural (and agricultural) reform. See Connecticut State Agricultural Society, *Transactions* (Hartford, 1855), 300.

15. Christine Stansell, *City of Women: Sex and Class in New York, 1789–1860* (New York, 1986), 111–12; Blewett, *Men, Women, and Work*, 99; Prude, *Coming of Industrial Order*, 122–23.

16. On industrial paternalism and inside contracting, see, respectively, Philip Scranton, "Varieties of Paternalism: Industrial Structures and the Social Relations of Production in American Textiles," *American Quarterly*,

36 (Summer 1984), 235–57; and Ernest J. Englander, "The Inside Contract System of Production and Organization: A Neglected Aspect of the History of the Firm," *Labor History*, 28 (Fall 1987), 429–46.

17. Dublin, *Women at Work*, chaps. 4–6; Prude, *Coming of Industrial Order*, 92–93; Stott, *Workers in the Metropolis*, 65–67.

18. Gary B. Nash, *Forging Freedom: The Formation of Philadelphia's Black Community, 1720–1840* (Cambridge, MA, 1988), 251; Teresa Ann Murphy, *Ten Hours' Labor: Religion, Reform, and Gender in Early New England* (Ithaca, 1992).

19. On deteriorating working conditions in textile mills, see Ware, *Early New England Cotton Manufacture*, 269–272; and Dublin, *Women at Work*, 90, 109–12, 203.

20. For an able inquiry into the wide variety of responses evinced by industrial laborers in this period, see David A. Zonderman, *Aspirations and Anxieties: New England Workers and the Mechanized Factory System, 1815–1850* (New York, 1992).

21. A dated but still informative treatment of antebellum labor and reform organizations and activism is found in Norman B. Ware, *The Industrial Worker, 1840–1860: the Reaction of American Industrial Society to the Advance of the Industrial Revolution* (Boston, 1924). Also see generally Wilentz, *Chants Democratic;* Murphy, *Ten Hours' Labor*, chap. 4; and Dublin, *Women at Work*, chaps. 4–6, 12. On shoemakers, see Blewett, *Men, Women, and Work*, 21, 33–43, and chap. 5.

22. The major threat of destruction came in the form of arson. See Gary Kulik "Pawtucket Village and the Strike of 1824: The Origin of Class Conflict in Rhode Island," in *Radical History Review*, 17 (Spring 1978), 5–37.

23. Prude, *Coming of Industrial Order*, chap. 5.

SIX

Artisans and Capitalist Development

RICHARD STOTT

TWENTY YEARS HAVE PASSED SINCE the publication of Alan Dawley's pathbreaking *Class and Community: The Industrial Revolution in Lynn* (1976), the first of a wave of studies that focused on artisans (also called craftsmen, tradesmen, and mechanics) in the nineteenth century.[1] Mechanics in virtually every major American city, and several minor ones, became the subject of historical examination.[2] Scholars have also studied specific trades.[3] This body of literature influenced and shaped historians' views on American industrialization, as a glance at any almost any college-level textbook will confirm. We now have a clear, coherent framework to interpret capitalism's impact on craftsmen, but this framework has come with some costs.[4]

Collectively, artisan historians portray capitalism as having a strongly adverse effect on craftsmen. While admitting tensions between masters and journeymen, scholars have generally depicted the preindustrial workshop in glowing terms. "From the day he signed on as an apprentice, the young artisan witnessed everyday democracy in action," writes Ronald Schultz, "working life in these settings was necessarily intimate and governed by overarching norms of mutuality and cooperation."[5] Sympathies are clearly with mechanics victimized by the onset of an exploitative, impersonal, market system. Their prime resource in resisting the decline of the small-shop world was their republican ideology.

Sean Wilentz's eloquent *Chants Democratic: New York City & the Rise of the American Working Class, 1788–1850* (1984) made republicanism the defining characteristic of artisans' lives. In his view mechanics were "sober, self-reliant, respectable men" who believed their own independence and virtue were responsible for creating the American republic.[6] The nation, these artisans held, should be governed by those most necessary to its progress: manual producers like themselves. Their model of an ideal political community was the harmony between masters and journeymen in the small shop. The market revolution was thus much more than merely an attack on artisans' standards of living; it was an assault on their perception of themselves as protectors of the American commonwealth. Protests by mechanics during early industrialization were less the result of narrow self-interest, declining working conditions, and lower wages, than the damage done to deeply held republican values.

Because many of these works have placed artisan republicanism at the heart of their story, they have come to constitute a historical paradigm. They eclipsed the older more materialistic interpretation of John R. Commons, the originator of the influential Wisconsin approach to labor history. Commons's framework, laid out in his noted article "American Shoemakers, 1648–1895," saw artisan protest as motivated by economic self-interest in response to expanding markets.[7] Commons's influential four-volume *History of Labour in the United States* (1919–1935) embodied this interpretation and along with Carl Bridenbaugh's *The Colonial Craftsman* (1950) was the pioneer work in the field.[8]

The powerful and influential artisan republican interpretation of recent years has furthered our understanding of mechanics' responses to the changes of the late eighteenth and early nineteenth century. Its dominance, however, has restricted important areas of research and has thus given an incomplete, even misleading, account. Although most of these artisan scholars see themselves as "new" labor historians examining the cultural milieu of work as well as the story of the labor movement, their approach has proved insufficiently broad to encompass the complex and sweeping reorganization of production that accompanied the transportation and industrial revolutions. Historians now know a great deal about artisan ideology, about politics and labor organizations, but far less about other aspects of artisans' lives. The problem is not that artisan republicanism is incorrect, but that it is simply too limited in scope to serve as a paradigm to comprehend the profound economic and social transformation of the early nineteenth century.

The emphasis on consciousness as exemplified in politics and unions has come at the expense of close descriptions of what the artisan work experience actually was like. Herbert Gutman helped launch the "new" labor history in his essay "Work, Culture and Society in Industrializing America, 1815–1919." Gutman's description of the workshop's informal labor discipline and sporadic work rhythms was so influential that subsequent historians saw little need for further elaboration, and they mostly turned out community studies of artisan republicanism that came to define the field.[9] Structural questions remained unanswered. Historians still only have a vague idea of timing, numbers involved, and fortunes of artisans in the early nineteenth century.[10] Because such major issues have not been researched satisfactorily, historians have relied on a preconceived, tragic, shop-breakdown model, and on the self-interested statements of artisans that reinforce this model.

One result of this approach is an overemphasis on urban artisans. America before the Civil War was overwhelmingly rural, and the vast majority of skilled craftsmen lived in the countryside: urban mechanics made up less than 5 percent of the nation's population. In Frederick County, Maryland, in 1820 only 520 of 3,015 "manufacturers" (who were mostly artisans) lived in Frederick City, one of the largest nonport towns in the United States.[11] Especially neglected have been southern artisans, both white and black. Bridenbaugh recognized their significance, but because the South was so rural, the region's craftsmen have been overlooked by most recent studies.[12] The comparative neglect of artisans in the countryside is especially disappointing since the widening markets of the early nineteenth century probably had their greatest impact on them. The literature is scanty in comparison with urban mechanics, but enough information exists to outline their history.[13]

Most artisans in the countryside, like their city counterparts, had always been involved in a market economy. Until the early nineteenth century, however, rural craftsmen were limited and protected by poor transport, as George Rogers Taylor explained in his *The Transportation Revolution, 1815–1860*, published in 1951 and still the best account of the market revolution.[14] Poor roads made it extremely expensive to ship goods very far in most inland areas. Rural producers thus had limited opportunity to compete outside their immediate market yet also were protected from outside competition. Each village, as in Taylor's famed Mount Pleasant, Ohio, in 1815, had its own manufacturing infrastructure of blacksmiths, gunsmiths, tailors, etc.[15] As transportation improved through the development of highways, canals, and railroads, these barriers began to come down. Simultaneously, farmers became more involved in commercial agriculture and increasingly purchased goods formerly made at home. With expanding local markets no longer limited to the immediate vicinity, some rural artisans adjusted their methods of production, reduced costs, and succeeded in the new economic environment.[16] But rural artisans also lost protection from long-distance competition, and cities with access to capital and large pools of labor usually could carry on manufacturing much more cheaply. Traditionally, men's coats were "cut up by the country retailer," and sewed by farm wives and daughters. After transportation costs declined, large ready-made clothing firms developed in New York and in other major cities. Because one skilled cutter could cut enough garments for three hundred sewers—usually low-paid German and Irish immigrants—city clothiers could furnish ready-made garments so cheaply "that the cost to the consumer is less than he was able to obtain by the old method, of purchasing the material and getting it made up at home." A "Country Tailor" complained to the New York *Daily Tribune*: "the wholesale clothing establishments . . . are forcing their work into the villages, along the rivers, canals, and railroads, absorbing the business of the country; and thus casting many an honest and hardworking man out of employment, or drawing them to your city by taking their work there. . . . It is thus that the large cities swallow up the small towns."[17]

This process of consolidation—which suggests that division-of-labor and not mechanization was at the heart of the industrial revolution—is one historians need to know much more about. It was coupled to the integration of farming into the market economy, as the work of Christopher Clark and Martin Bruegel makes clear.[18]

It also connected rural and urban artisans: economic expansion increased the demand for skilled workers in urban areas, and, as the "Country Tailor" suggests, some former rural artisans ended up in cities. How many artisans moved to the city? Did they do well there? And what of those artisans who stayed behind in the countryside? Did they increasingly specialize in custom and repair work? What was their economic fate?[19] These questions concerning rural craftsmen have been deflected by the artisan-republican paradigm and the emphasis on the urban scene.

Even when we turn to the artisan in the city, we see that despite almost a generation of intensive research, important issues remain unresolved. The focus on urban industrialization, artisan republicanism, and the erosion of the traditional master-journeyman-apprentice craft-based system led historians to broad, simplistic, and misleading generalizations. Charles Sellers, for instance, asserted that "the commercial boom had inaugurated an irreversible proletarianization of the mechanic class."[20] In trades such as shoemaking (the trade that, following Commons and Dawley, has been the main historical model for the impact of industrialization on artisans), there was a trend toward factory manufacturing, with a devastating impact on artisan shoemakers. Yet most skilled trades did not decline as dramatically—a number even flourished.

Several crafts were largely unaffected by change during the early nineteenth century, especially the construction trades. Plastering remained almost the same from the eighteenth century until the introduction of prefabricated laths in the late nineteenth century.[21] In addition, new skilled trades such as plumber and machinist emerged in the first half of the nineteenth century. Even more important than uneven development among trades were the variations *within* trades. Economist Michael J. Piore has divided manufacturing into a "primary" sector meeting steady demand for standardized products with machinery, and a "secondary" sector filling fashionable, specialized, or variable demand through labor-intensive, often skilled, techniques.[22] Within almost every trade there developed mechanics producing to fill limited, nonstandardized, demand. Philip Scranton has analyzed this part of the industrial revolution for textiles. In comparison to the huge mills of Lowell, Scranton describes in Philadelphia a "coherent alternative manufacturing system," with small mill owners "applying their craft talents in individual partial process firms reliant on skilled labor to generate a diverse array of seasonal specialties rather than staple textiles." The number of handlooms and handloom weavers actually increased in Philadelphia in the 1850s.[23]

Printing underwent a similar transformation. In the eighteenth century, masters printed everything—newspapers, books, and advertising circulars. As demand skyrocketed the trade specialized: high-speed steam-powered rotary presses printed newspapers and books. Such presses, however, had expensive set-up and energy costs and were only economical for long runs. To meet demand for small runs of handbills, cards, and other customized products, the separate specialty of job printing emerged using foot-powered presses and relying on skilled printers. Furniture manufacturing also segmented. Master cabinetmakers in the early 1800s, men such as Duncan Phyfe, made a variety of furniture in a range of prices. In the mid-nineteenth century, "slaughter shops" in cities like New York began using intensive division-of-labor with semi-trained workers called "botches" to produce cheap chairs. Simultaneously, other establishments began specializing in expensive, highly-crafted "imperial" furniture using trained, well-paid craftsmen.[24]

Such complexity undercuts attempts by historians to comprehend the impact of the industrial revolution by "proletarianization."[25] Growing division-of-labor probably decreased the percentage of highly skilled manual workers in the labor force, but the huge increase in production meant that the demand for well-paid skilled craft workers was growing. In New York City in 1805 there were about 200 cabinetmakers, most of whom were highly trained. By 1853 there were 4,000 cabinetmakers in the city—twenty times as many—of whom about 800 were highly skilled.[26]

In comprehending the effect of labor market segmentation, mobility studies are helpful. Perhaps the most interesting of these works is Clyde and Sally Griffen's *Natives and Newcomers: The Ordering of Opportunity in Mid-Nineteenth-Century Poughkeepsie.* Although in some Poughkeepsie trades skilled artisans saw their skills undermined, overall "old and new in organization, methods, and outlook coexisted through much of the period in many manufacturing crafts. . . . Change in individual crafts in Poughkeepsie as in other localities sometimes reversed national patterns," as some firms shrank and began to meet local custom demand by using skilled craftsmen. The changes caused by the industrial revolution in Poughkeepsie were complicated—there were artisans who gained as well as artisans who lost.[27]

The experience of Philadelphia weavers, New York printers, and Poughkeepsie craftsmen suggests how misleading it is to rely simply on the shoemaker-inspired decline-of-the-artisan model. Although small shops no longer were as central to the manufacturing process as they had been in the eighteenth century—many now engaged in specialty and repair work—they continued to thrive. In the 1860 census there were on average only 9.3 employees per manufacturing firm; even in New England the average was only 19.0.[28] It is my guess that during industrialization the great majority of artisans found work in the skilled, small shop sector of their trade, or worked in large factories either as foremen or in skilled manual positions (such as the cutters in the clothing industry).[29] Not many mechanics ended as factory operatives. The Griffens found few artisans in Poughkeepsie's factories: most employees were immigrants. In New York City also, the vast bulk of unskilled and semiskilled workers were Irish and German immigrants.

In England changes in living standards became central in evaluating the impact of industrialization.[30] Surprisingly, there has not been comparable discussion and research for American industrialization. (Mobility studies like the Griffens' examine occupation, not income.) Generally, American historians of artisans have been more interested in consciousness and have agreed with E. P. Thompson that what was at stake was "the total life experience" of artisans rather than merely material well-being.[31] Most of these scholars assume—based largely on statements of protesting artisans—that living standards did decline; this, however, has not been a major topic of research.[32] Yet, economic historians believe that there was a significant increase in per capita income in the antebellum period. Could all of it have gone to the bosses?[33] Living standards need more investigation, especially such concrete subjects as diet and housing. Billy G. Smith portrays eighteenth-century Philadelphia artisans as hovering on the edge of poverty and concludes that "the preindustrial period was not a golden age. . . . Perhaps the negative changes wrought by the factory have been overestimated, the deleterious impact exaggerated."[34]

Most artisans may not have suffered because of the economic

changes of early 1800s; many, perhaps even most, gained. I am not denying that there were clear losers, but we cannot base our understanding of industrialization exclusively on their experience. Economic growth created many highly skilled, well-paying jobs. Surely the number was several times greater than had existed in preindustrial America. Many shoemakers saw their livelihood destroyed, but plumbers, plasterers, and imperial furniture makers thrived.

If some historians have exaggerated the negative impact of the market revolution, they have also tended to idealize preindustrial society. It is the ambience of the small shop that is in the forefront of the historical literature, rather than work or wages. Although most labor historians deny a preindustrial golden age, the general picture is extremely positive, emphasizing the mutuality of the workshop in comparison to the antagonism of the factory and sweatshop. But in reality was that way of life really so ideal? Artisans themselves were far more ambiguous about the small-shop world than contemporary historians. In public statements mechanics often referred to a lost age of workshop harmony, but artisan autobiographies and reminiscences paint a different picture.[35]

Was being a master really so significant? Achieving that status became harder in the nineteenth century. Lisa Beth Lubow's study of Boston carpenters shows that 45 percent of journeymen in 1790 became masters in the city; by 1825 that number had fallen to 11 percent.[36] Still, becoming a boss was far from impossible, given the durability of the small shop. Capital requirements were increasing, but in many crafts shop owning was still within reach, especially if a journeyman was willing to go into partnership.[37]

When a journeymen did become a master, he often found himself in a difficult and demanding situation. Historians may be overly impressed with the term "master," with its image of men like Paul Revere and Duncan Phyfe. There have been studies of successful masters, but little attention has been paid to less fortunate, struggling masters.[38] Many operated on a shoestring. In the 1820s "Caleb Snug," a journeyman Connecticut coachmaker "infatuated with the idea of becoming boss," quickly became disillusioned when he set up his own shop. "Boss coachmakers had their troubles. . . . While a journeyman, when the day's work was over, my mind was freed from care and business. Not so now." Especially bothersome was trying to collect debts from deadbeat, even swindling, customers. Snug concluded that the "business . . . is burthened with perplexities enough to discourage most persons under the most careful management."[39]

Apprentices and journeymen found some masters kind, others cruel; some workshops cordial, others unpleasant. Apprentices were particularly vulnerable to the vagaries of the master since they were legally bound to remain for three to five years.[40] "Many hogs were better fed and housed," complained James Bogart of his 1802 New York City apprenticeship in printing.[41] In Lynn, Massachusetts, apprentice shoemakers were "generally flogged" for their misbehavior.[42] Journeymen were better off, but many complained about being cheated in pay and made to work too long. Yet the possibilities of protest were limited; most apprentices lived with masters, as did some journeymen (though the latter was never the general practice). The master and journeymen ate noon dinner together in the shop, and outside of work they usually lived near each other, since there was a considerable intermixture of ranks in the preindustrial city.[43] In such a personalized situation, opposition took rudimentary and oblique forms. In a Saugatuck, Connecticut, coachmaking shop in 1816, the apprentices and journeymen protested their diet of "pork and potatoes to-day, potatoes and pork to-morrow," by anonymously chalking "PORK" on the shop wall. The master, infuriated, threatened to jam the person who wrote on the wall "against 'them stairs.'" The intimidated employees all denied responsibility.[44]

If the small shop world was less pleasant than it is often portrayed, and most artisans did not have their chances for success ended by the transportation and industrial revolution, how can we explain the widespread protests of the 1820s and 1830s? Journeymen insisted things were getting worse. Why should we not believe them? Obviously these are critical questions, since these protests stand as "Exhibit A" for the declension model. In trades like shoemaking things were getting worse. But historians working within the artisan republican framework have underestimated the way social changes associated with industrialization allowed employees to more easily mobilize opposition. The breakdown of the personalized master-journeyman relationship in larger shops and

the growth of neighborhoods and institutions such as taverns occupied entirely by employees strengthened journeymen's solidarity.[45] Historians investigating workers in the early twentieth century, such as Lizabeth Cohen, have shown how fruitful it can be to
examine the ways industrialization empowered employees.[46] A similar emphasis for the early nineteenth century should prove fruitful. Perhaps protests were muted in the preindustrial period because the artisan system constituted a *more* effective form of
subordination than the factory system; perhaps for some artisans
industrialization was a liberation.

The transportation revolution disrupted the artisans' world,
but that world was not so ideal as it has been portrayed. As old
opportunities and solidarities disappeared, new ones emerged. The
existing literature, with its emphasis on decline and republicanism, has told part of the story. But there is much more. Even in the
realm of consciousness, the artisan republican emphasis has slighted
religion and popular culture. There is some information on the
influence of Protestantism on craftsmen, but religion still needs to
be situated more effectively within artisan life.[47] There has also
been important work on reading in the early republic; this too
could be integrated into a more comprehensive picture of artisans.[48]

What is needed, then, is not more "new" labor history of artisans centered on the declension model and republicanism, but a
return to the original intent of the "new" labor history to provide
the economic, social, and cultural context of the artisans in both
city and country. Historians need to know much more about the
realities of the artisan system, the concrete impact of industrialization on mechanics, and the ensuing social and cultural changes.
Investigating the varied aspects of artisan life will present historians a more realistic, and perhaps more human, class of artisans
than that of the existing literature.

NOTES

1. Alan Dawley, *Class and Community: The Industrial Revolution in Lynn*
(Cambridge, MA, 1976). The term "artisan" was not widely used in the
eighteenth and nineteenth centuries. Skilled, male craftsmen, however,

were spoken of as a group in this period: the more common term was "mechanics."

2. Although dealing with the colonial period, Gary B. Nash, *The Urban Crucible: Social Change, Political Consciousness, and the Origins of the American Revolution* (Cambridge, MA, 1979), has been influential in historical treatments of postrevolutionary artisans. For general literature on artisans in the early republic period, see notes 17 and 18 in Paul A. Gilje, "The Rise of Capitalism," in this volume. On smaller towns see Thomas R. Winpenny, *Bending is Not Breaking: Adaption and Persistence Among Nineteenth-Century Lancaster Artisans* (Lanham, MD, 1990); and Carol N. Toner, *Persisting Traditions: Artisan Work and Culture in Bangor, Maine, 1828–1868* (New York, 1995). Sometimes dubbed the "new labor history" in contrast to the Wisconsin school (see below), these works now seem rather traditional with their focus on protest as embodied in politics and unions and their scanty treatment of women and blacks—perhaps not so different from the old labor history after all. This literature is excellently summarized in Bruce Laurie, *Artisans into Workers: Labor in Nineteenth-Century America* (New York, 1989).

3. David Bensman, *The Practice of Solidarity: American Hat Finishers in the Nineteenth Century* (Urbana, 1985); William Stanley Pretzer, "Printers of Washington, D. C., 1800–1880: Work, Culture, Technology and Trade Unionism," (Ph.D. diss., Northern Illinois University, 1986); Lisa Beth Lubow, "Artisans in Transition: Early Capitalist Development and the Carpenters of Boston, 1787–1837," (Ph.D. diss., University of California, Los Angeles, 1987).

4. By emphasizing the similar themes of these studies, I do not mean to minimize the considerable differences among these historians. However, I do feel that there is enough commonality to speak of them as a group.

5. Ronald Schultz, *The Republic of Labor: Philadelphia Artisans and the Politics of Class, 1720–1830* (New York, 1993), 6, 7.

6. Sean Wilentz, *Chants Democratic: New York City & the Rise of the American Working Class, 1788–1850* (New York, 1984), 58.

7. John R. Commons, "American Shoemakers, 1648–1895," in Commons, *Labor and Administration* (New York, 1913), 219–66. Commons's approach is too schematic to be very usable to historians, but his emphasis on economics and market extension is sound.

8. John R. Commons *et al., History of Labour in the United States* (4 vols., New York, 1918–1935); Carl Bridenbaugh, *The Colonial Craftsman* (1950; rep., Chicago, 1974). By looking at artisans, both Commons and new labor historians like Dawley were forsaking a traditional Marxist-influenced approach that tended to focus on factory workers in the early industrial revolution. This difference in emphasis is seen by comparison

to Norman Ware's *The Industrial Worker, 1840–1860* (1924; rep., Chicago, 1990).

9. Herbert Gutman, "Work, Culture and Society in Industrializing America, 1815–1919," in Gutman, *Work, Culture and Society in Industrializing America: Essays in American Working-Class History* (New York, 1976), esp. 32–54.

10. The only demographic study is Susan E. Klepp, *Philadelphia in Transition: A Demographic History of the City and its Occupational Groups, 1720–1830* (New York, 1989).

11. Census Office, *Census for 1820* (Washington, DC, 1821).

12. A recent collection of essays on artisans edited by Howard B. Rock, Paul A. Gilje, and Robert Asher, eds., *American Artisans: Crafting Social Identity, 1750–1850* (Baltimore, 1995) suggests that the neglect of southern artisans may be ending. This work contains informative essays on craftsmen in the South by Christine Daniels, Tina H. Sheller, Michele K. Gillespie, and James Sidbury.

13. One difficulty is, of course, that evidence on dispersed rural artisans is much harder to discover than on their urban counterparts who formed associations, marched in parades, and founded newspapers. It is possible, however, to tell the story of mechanics outside urban areas. One interesting study is Charles F. Hummel, *With Hammer in Hand: The Dominy Craftsmen of East Hampton, New York* (Charlottesville, 1968). Hummel's book is a fine example of what might be dubbed the "Winterthur School" of artisan history. These studies, done in association with the Winterthur Museum, focus more on work*ing* and less on work*ers* than the labor histories. For a good introduction, see Ian M. G. Quimby, ed., *The Craftsman in Early America* (New York, 1984).

14. George Rogers Taylor, *The Transportation Revolution, 1815–1860* (New York, 1951), esp. 207–10.

15. It is symptomatic of the neglect of rural craftsmen that the most numerous trade in the countryside, the ubiquitous blacksmith, has received such little historical attention. For an excellent recent treatment, see Christine Daniels, "'WANTED: A Blacksmith who understands Plantation Work': Artisans in Maryland, 1700–1810," *William and Mary Quarterly*, 50 (Oct. 1993), 743–67. Daniels's approach could serve as a model for future studies of rural craftsmen.

16. David Jaffee believes that the "market economy . . . injected new vitality into at least some traditional rural handicrafts." Jaffee, "One of the Primitive Sort: Portrait Makers of the Rural North," in Steven Hahn and Jonathan Prude, eds., *The Countryside in the Age of Capitalist Transformation: Essays in the Social History of the Rural North* (Chapel Hill, 1985), 103.

17. *United States Economist and Dry Goods Reporter* (New York), Nov.

6, 1852; *ibid.*, Feb. 26, 1853; "Letter from a COUNTRY TAILOR," New York *Daily Tribune*, June 16, 1849.

18. Christopher Clark, *The Roots of Rural Capitalism: Western Massachusetts, 1780–1860* (Ithaca, 1990), 94–101; Martin Bruegel, "The Rise of a Market Society in the Rural Hudson Valley," (Ph. D. diss., Cornell University, 1994), 215–79.

19. In the Hudson Valley, artisans remained between 15 and 20 percent of the labor force in the antebellum period, even as the farm population declined and the factory population grew; Bruegel, "Rise of a Market Society," 222–23.

20. Charles G. Sellers, *The Market Revolution: Jacksonian America, 1815–1846* (New York, 1991), 25.

21. Harley J. McKee, *Introduction to Early American Masonry: Stone, Brick, Mortar and Plaster* (Washington, DC, 1973), 81–89. The continued reliance on skilled, manual labor in English construction is emphasized in Raphael Samuel, "Workshop of the World: Steam Power and Hand Technology in mid-Victorian Britain," *History Workshop*, 3 (Spring 1977), 27–32. A similar study of the nineteenth-century American construction workers—who have been largely ignored by labor historians—would be valuable.

22. Michael J. Piore, *Birds of Passage: Migrant Labor and Industrial Society* (New York, 1979), 35–43. Piore's argument seems to me essential for comprehending the diversity of the impact of the industrial revolution. For a wide-ranging historical application of Piore's theory, see Charles Sabel and Theodore Zeitlin, "Historical Alternatives to Mass Production: Politics, Markets, and Technology in Nineteenth-Century Industrialization," *Past and Present*, 108 (Aug. 1985), 133–76.

23. Philip Scranton, *Figured Tapestry: Production, Markets, and Power in Philadelphia Textiles,1885–1941* (Cambridge, 1989), 1; and Scranton, *Proprietary Capitalism: The Textile Manufacture at Philadelphia, 1800–1885* (Cambridge, 1983), 220–21.

24. On printing, see Richard B. Stott, *Workers in the Metropolis: Class, Ethnicity, and Youth in Antebellum New York City* (Ithaca, 1990), 20–23, 48–55. On furniture, see Stott, "Furniture Manufacturing," in Kenneth Jackson, ed., *The Encyclopedia of New York City* (New Haven, 1995). Philip Scranton analyzes the segmentation in the jewelry and machine tool industries for a later period in "Diversity in Diversity: Flexible Production and American Industrialization," *Business History Review*, 65 (Spring 1991), 27–90.

25. The enormous complexity of industrialization is emphasized in Walter Licht, *Industrializing America: The Nineteenth Century* (Baltimore, 1995).

26. Cabinetmakers estimated from Howard B. Rock, *Artisans of the New Republic: The Tradesman of New York City in the Age of Jefferson* (New York, 1979), 12–13; and New York (NY) *Herald,* June 18, 1853. In New York City, the average workplace actually became *smaller* in the nineteenth century as Manhattan became specialized within the metropolitan manufacturing region as the center for batch and customized production. In 1820 the incomplete manufacturing census showed an average of 14.7 employees per shop, by 1860 it grew to 20.6, by 1900 it had declined to 13.9; Stott, *Workers in the Metropolis,* 28.

27. Clyde and Sally Griffen, *Natives and Newcomers: The Ordering of Opportunity in Mid-Nineteenth-Century Poughkeepsie* (Cambridge, MA, 1978), 142. Unfortunately, the 1850 census is the first to ask about occupation, so mobility studies can examine only the latter part of the market revolution. The Poughkeepsie example is reinforced by the only regional economic study I have seen: Timothy E. Sullivan, "The Transformation and Integration of the American Manufacturing Frontier: The Midwest from 1850–1880," (Ph.D. diss., University of Illinois, 1987), 98, "Small-scale artisan production continued to play a significant role throughout the mid-nineteenth century"—during the period about one half of all manufacturing establishments were artisan shops and there was no evidence of decline.

28. Even in 1890 the average national manufacturing workplace size was only 13.3 employees; Census Office, Twelfth Census, 1900, *Manufactures—Part I* (Washington, DC, 1903), xxxlv.

29. The transition from artisan to foreman for a printer is traced in William S. Pretzer's study, "From Artisan to Alderman: The Career of William W. Moore, 1803–1886," in Rock, Gilje and Asher, eds., *American Artisans,* 135–52.

30. Arthur John Taylor, ed., *The Standard of Living in Britain in the Industrial Revolution* (London, 1975).

31. E. P. Thompson, *The Making of the English Working Class* (New York, 1963), 444.

32. Steven J. Ross, for example, believes "the working class, taken as a whole—at least in Cincinnati—never regained the widespread prosperity" of the early nineteenth century; Ross, *Workers On the Edge: Work, Leisure, and Politics in Industralizing Cincinnati, 1788–1890* (New York, 1985), 9.

33. For a fine overview and analysis of these economic studies, see Kenneth Sokoloff and Georgia C. Villaflor, "The Market for Manufacturing Workers During Early Industrialization: The American Northeast, 1820–1860," in Claudia Goldin and Hugh Rockoff, eds., *Strategic Factors in Nineteenth Century American Economic History: A Volume to Honor Robert W. Fogel* (Chicago, 1992), 29–62. Their conclusion is that "all of the groups distinguishable in our data received substantial increases in real wages

... from 1820 to 1860. ... Wages [of traditional artisans] grew more rapidly than those of other manufacturing workers," Sokoloff and Villaflor, "The Market for Manufacturing Workers," 61. However, Jeffrey G. Williamson and Peter H. Lindert, *American Inequality: A Macroeconomic History* (New York, 1980), argue that rising per capita income was accompanied by rising inequality. One problem in works by both labor and economic historians is their focus on daily and weekly wages. Regularity of employment in the seasonal economy of the early nineteenth century was probably more important than wage rates in determining yearly income.

34. Billy G. Smith, *The "Lower Sort": Philadelphia's Laboring People, 1750–1800* (Ithaca, 1990), 200. The only similar study is Peter Shergold's *Working Class Life: The "American Standard" in Comparative Perspective, 1899–1913* (Pittsburgh, 1982). Thus, the entire nineteenth century is missed.

35. This generalization is based largely on the following first-person accounts, which are the best I have read: Edward Thomas Day, *The Andrus Bindery—A History of the Shop, 1831–1838*, ed. Newton C. Brainard (Hartford, Conn., 1940) (bookbinding); David N. Johnson, *Sketches of Lynn* (1880; rep. Westport, Conn., 1970) (shoemaking); William Otter, Sr., *History of My Own Times*, ed. Richard B. Stott (1835; rep. Ithaca, 1995) (plastering); Samuel Seabury, *Moneygripe's Apprentice: The Personal Narrative of Samuel Seabury III*, ed. Robert Bruce Mullin (New Haven, 1989) (cabinetmaking); "The Autobiography of Caleb Snug, of Snugtown, Carriage-Maker," *New York Coachmaker's Magazine*, II–III (1859–1861) (although the names are comic, this is clearly based on a real apprenticeship); and Ebenezer Hiram Stedman, *Bluegrass Craftsman: Being the Reminiscences of Ebenezer Hiram Stedman, 1808–1885*, ed. Francis L. S. Dugan and Jacqueline P. Bull (Lexington, 1959) (papermaking, pottery making, iron molding). The numerous nineteenth-century artisan autobiographies, I believe, provide a truer picture of artisanal life than public statements and could help provide the basis for future studies.

36. Lubow, "Artisans in Transition," 199, 209.

37. Interesting information on the process by which manual workers became bosses in the 1850s is found in the R. G. Dun and Company Collection, (Baker Library, Harvard Graduate School of Business Administration, Cambridge, MA).

38. A fine study of successful artisans is Gary John Kornblith, "From Artisans to Businessmen: Master Mechanics in New England," (Ph.D. diss., Princeton University, 1983); see also Gutman, *Work, Culture and Society in Industrializing America*, 211–33.

39. "Autobiography of Caleb Snug," *New York Coachmen's Magazine*, III (Nov. 1860), 109, 110; *ibid.*, III (May, 1861), 222.

40. William J. Rorabaugh, *The Craft Apprentice: From Franklin to the Machine Age in America* (New York, 1986), is a very thorough study.

41. Bogart quoted in Milton W. Hamilton, *The Country Printer: New York State, 1785–1839* (New York, 1936), 36.

42. Johnson, *Sketches of Lynn*, 63.

43. Elizabeth Blackmar, *Manhattan for Rent, 1785–1850* (Ithaca, 1989).

44. "Autobiography of Caleb Snug," *New York Coachmaker's Magazine*, II (Oct., Nov. 1859), 82, 101–02. At Silas Andrus's Hartford, Connecticut bookbindery, the employees agreed to refuse to work more than eleven hours during the summer; one of the bosses ordered them back to work, threatening to "knock them down with an iron bar" if any left; none did. Day, *The Andrus Bindery*, 23. This was somewhat bigger than most traditional artisan bookbinderies, having twelve employees.

45. Stuart M. Blumin, *The Emergence of the Middle Class: Social Experience in the American City, 1760–1900* (Cambridge, 1989), 83–91, notes the increasing physical separation, even within small shops, of manual and nonmanual workers in the first half of the nineteenth century.

46. Lizabeth Cohen, *Making A New Deal: Industrial Workers in Chicago, 1919–1939* (Cambridge, 1990). See also Roy Rosenzweig, *Eight Hours for What We Will: Workers and Leisure in an Industrial City* (Cambridge, 1983).

47. Material on the religious views of artisans can be found in Laurie, *Working People of Philadelphia*; Wilentz, *Chants Democratic*; Paul G. Faler, *Mechanics and Manufacturers in the Early Industrial Revolution: Lynn, Massachusetts, 1760–1860* (Albany, 1981); Charles G. Steffen, *The Mechanics of Baltimore: Workers and Politics in the Age of the Revolution, 1763–1812* (Urbana, 1984): Teresa Ann Murphy, *Ten Hours' Labor: Religion, Reform and Gender in Early New England* (Ithaca, 1992); and Jama Lazerow, *Religion and the Working Class in Antebellum America* (Washington, DC, 1995).

48. William J. Gilmore, *Reading Becomes a Necessity of Life: Material and Cultural Life in Rural New England, 1780–1835* (Knoxville, 1989); Ronald Zboray, *A Fictive People: Antebellum Economic Development and the American Reading Public* (New York, 1993).

SEVEN

Capitalizing Hope:
Economic Thought and
the Early National Economy

CATHY D. MATSON

GREAT NUMBERS OF EARLY NATIONAL Americans were convinced that their potential for material prosperity was unequaled anywhere else on earth. After all, as colonists they had enjoyed protected markets and encouragement of shipping under the regulatory hand of what Adam Smith later called "mercantilism." Their own pragmatic experience in the individual colonies also taught them how to legislate schemes for new kinds of taxation, currency, trade routes, and manufactures. Then, the American Revolution seemed to release their energies further, encouraging people to improve, produce, and consume more, even as it demanded public sacrifice. In the new states, Americans experimented boldly in centralized banking and currency emission, which in turn aided farmers and merchant exporters with inflationary paper money. Some observers proposed that money embodied not only present circulating goods and labor but the potential for development as well. Writings about the immanent prosperity of millsites, forges, and stores in the hinterlands flourished in the final revolutionary months, and habits of indebtedness and risk-taking foreshadowed the great appeal of a nationally self-sufficient political economy.[1]

But what policies and market relations would stimulate and sustain this economic promise? Exactly how should Americans capitalize hope? By the 1770s many writers believed that poverty and scarcities were not reliable external spurs to enterprising labor; traditional injunctions to keep wages and interest rates low did not necessarily inspire productive energies. Perhaps, reasoned some observers, the pace of material change would quicken if individuals detached their economic freedoms from concerns about the traditional community or polity; perhaps Calvinism's and the Scottish Enlightenment's appeal to an inner moral sense would be adequate to tame the excesses of liberated self-interest. These voices coexisted with the chorus of writers who persisted in the view that furthering, protecting, and limiting private economic interests required a stable political regime that regulated the economy. Indeed, tests of both intellectual heritages came during the economic trauma of the 1780s, a decade that historians have been rediscovering in recent years.[2] As the postwar flood of cheap English goods and long English credit came quickly to an end, northern states raised taxes on the property of middling landowners, the money supply contracted, debts went unpaid, investment in new lands and enterprises diminished, states discriminated against each other in trade, a depression rocked farm prices and urban employment, and there was a portent of debtor rebellions throughout the hinterlands.[3]

A central dilemma faced the nationalist leaders of the new United States: if participation in markets was to be free from attachment to inherited estates and privilege, free for all individuals to enjoy, then what role would there be for political authority? How might they structure politics and policymaking to eliminate the mutually annihilating tendencies of state and local governments, and still release economic energy? Their answer lay in the conferral by the new Constitution of a national political structure with the authority to create a uniform commerce and steady revenue. This new government would protect and extend the mutual interests of citizens whose markets were linked to cooperation in a world of hostile nations. It would also sanction a single currency, safeguard contracts, standardize business practices, patent inventions, and naturalize immigrants.[4] The urgent tasks of securing the economic institutions of the new nation drew writers of the postconstitutional generation into a vortex of treatise-writing and journalism. These authors borrowed from English and European ideas on political economy to help protect private property rights, validate the lending of money at interest, promote land sales for profit, and hasten the creation of a widespread free labor market alongside expanding slavery.[5]

Historians have analyzed this founding drama in great detail as well as its continuing impact on early national economic developments. Less well-documented, however, is the parallel public discussion extolling voluntarism, free will, and the harmony of unfettered economic agents in a web of markets. This second kind of optimism had the potential to coexist comfortably with the Federalist plan at certain moments, but it also created intellectual and policy challenges during the next generation's debate about its economic future. That debate centered on four vital areas of concern. Americans argued over the role of *land* as a repository for republican virtue and as a commodity in an expanding economy. They disputed the best means to release *commercial* energies and how to regulate them. In addition, new ideas appeared concerning *credit and banking* that formed yet another area of division. Finally, innovations in *internal improvements and manufacturing* elicited new formulations about America's future political economy.

Optimists invested great emotional capital in land, especially in the context of insisting that individual proprietorship provided a basis for family farms. Agriculture was the source of all true value according to Physiocratic arguments, and the availability of land offered an escape from the horror of overpopulation. In the American republic, the independence of the family farm also provided support for shunning the fiscal proposals of Federalists and bolstered prospects for unbroken demographic increase, unlimited natural bounty, and unfettered entrepreneurial improvement. Land had long been more than an environment for conferring republican values; it was also a commodity to buy and sell, as promoters of the great land companies so clearly demonstrated and reservation policies later ratified. Even on family farms production was becoming market-based, reliant on cash and credit relations, and separated from the traditional activities of household labor. Farming required a variety of skills associated with replacing and expanding household goods, milling, smithing, carpentry, childrearing, processing dairy and meat products, all of which drew the rural majority of the population into an intricate network of marketing, lending, cooperating, and hiring of labor at increasing distances. Contemporaries began to envision the hinterlands less as a terrain filling with self-sufficient farms than as "the greatest factory of American raw materials," yielding up substantial amounts of goods "for the use of other parts of the union." Theorists and state boosters alike enlarged definitions of "wealth" to include not only the general abundance around settlers, but the potential to transform nature into desirable goods, and to sell them to grocers, retailers, and small manufacturers involved in the "natural commerce" of the interior. Untransformed wilderness was just as much an obstacle to progress as a crowded, impoverished city. Family farms would become business enterprises and businessmen in rural stores would become stewards of the public will and welfare. The entire scenario often was premised on the complementarity of freely competing producers and supportive government laws and resources.[6] Some thoughtful commentators hitched their optimism to westward expansion, as when James Madison believed that migration over space, combined with policies related to commercial reciprocity, would spare Americans from the degrading effects of imported luxuries. Toward the end of his life, Madison grew even more hopeful that as the population rose from 3.9 million in 1790 to 9.6 million in 1830, including the addition of new states and Louisiana Territory, the West would also absorb vast numbers of migrants from eastern states, thereby permitting higher wages and better living standards for those who stayed behind in the cities.[7]

A competing view—then and now—suggests that city and country interests were less integrated. By 1789 northern Americans had recovered from low levels of revolutionary commerce, but even as the flow of goods into the country grew until 1807 (when the Jeffersonian embargoes prompted a commercial collapse) exchanges between eastern and western regions and production of semi-finished craft wares did not rise significantly in most places.[8] From 1807 to the 1820s putting-out experiments linked merchant capitalists with small producers of rural areas, but repeated crises of production and prices stifled the ability of many struggling urban Americans to integrate exchanges with the countryside. Further, migrating people consumed much of the increased production of agricultural and small craft commodities when they entered rural communities, and western farm output was not sufficient to meet coastal demand. Until the 1830s industrialization, with its attendant dislocations between labor and capital, public institutions associated with the promotion of national wealth, and greater articulation of regional markets, had barely touched most areas where commercial agriculture, paternal labor relations, and petty proprietorships prevailed. Aside from the rapidly changing mid-Atlantic milling and commercial farming regions, a substantial population of Americans set back from major waterways beyond the Mohawk and Susquehanna valleys produced for household use and local exchange; cash exchanges still were not pervasive in the areas experiencing the greatest pull on local production for international markets, and private savings and investment outside of the small circles of urban elites remained low. The story of cotton's boom lay largely after 1815.[9]

This same view that emphasizes enduring traditions over rapid changes in land relations, permits historians to test assumptions about rural market behavior. In brief, the profits from market sales, enhanced by new methods of mixed farming and the introduction of labor-saving machinery, may not have been pursued in the interests of emulating urban lifestyles; rather, they may have provided the means to sustain time-worn traditions of family farming or add to existing landholdings. Farm prices fluctuated, manufactured goods trickled unevenly into the countryside, farm labor remained expensive, and the burden of rural taxation could offset the rising prices farmers expected for commodities they sold to distant hungry Americans. Even the most prescient political economists such as Mathew Carey (1760–1839) overlooked the unevenness of development, including the simple fact that somewhere between one-quarter and one-half of rural families in newly opened lands were not proprietors of the idealized homestead, but were landless or tenants on poor soil. In short, the constitutional founders' hopes for a national market had no immediate or widespread satisfactory results.

Contemporary congressional and state leaders understood, as historians since then do, that commerce played a central role in the early national American economy. Here, too, conceptual differences arose. Many writers promoted commercial reciprocity, world peace, and freedom of the seas, but most recognized that England continued to be the primary market for American exports and investment capital, and with renewed warfare during the 1790s they understood that neo-mercantile policies were most suited to immediate commercial needs. The states persistently responded to commercial interests in the two decades following constitutional ratification, and the Napoleonic Wars drew traders into international diplomacy and prices as never before. This development hastened a shift from tobacco to grain production in the mid-Atlantic, and promoted efforts to raise prices for the meat, lumber, fish, and flour farmers had been exporting for decades. Overall, exports and earnings in the carrying trades rose about six-fold from 1790 to 1807, and imports rose commensurately to 1802 and then again in 1811–1812. New England shipbuilders boasted stable incomes from their carrying trade and sales of vessels to belligerents, while West Indies merchants tried new ports of call.[10]

Years later commerce still occupied a primary place in the economy for many contemporary observers. In 1825 John McVickar (1787–1868), one of the country's few paid teachers of political economy, spoke to the expanding generation of urban merchants whose competitive aloofness from each other got a fresh coat of Protestant varnish, for McVickar "reverence[d] the claims of commerce as something holy."[11] Others believed that correctives to commercial excesses would arise naturally when men "from the homes of decent competence or struggling poverty" attempted trade; indeed, commerce offered the antidote for "dwarfing or deforming tendencies" present in manual labor and might even "melt down the walls of estrangement which separate the various communities of mankind." Still others argued that not international but domestic trade was "the purest commerce," for it absorbed the greatest numbers of Americans into producing, circulating, and consuming daily needs.[12]

If this emphasis on commerce included a wide variety of approaches, a key question still remained: how much entrepreneurial freedom and how much government regulation was appropriate for commercial greatness? After the battles for uniform import duties to create a federal revenue and overcome interstate quarrels in the 1790s, new voices came forward to demand that the principle of commercial regulation be extended in protectionism. Mathew Carey and many of his peers reversed the arguments of a previous generation. Instead of a regulated internal economy and freedom of the seas, they insisted upon relatively high tariffs walls, to protect and extend the sphere of justice for Americans in a world of hostile nations and monopoly interests. Simultaneously, they pleaded for government to preserve as much liberty of movement and investment for individuals within the nation as it possibly could, thereby promoting widespread consumption of new wants among the "improving middle." Moving beyond the pessimistic forecasts of Malthus and Ricardo, who foresaw cycles of aggressive competition and then widespread scarcities, Carey plus a handful of labor radicals and larger numbers of small manufacturers, canal promoters, mill operators, and commercial farmers ranged themselves against southern support for free trade in the first decades of the nineteenth century.[13]

Combinations of merchants and manufacturers who needed capital and labor for domestic manufacturing redoubled their efforts to get special protective measures passed by state governments, while skilled craftsmen agreed that higher tariffs would stimulate demand for their craft and housebuilding skills. By the Panic of 1819 much northern writing associated Adam Smith with free importation that corrupted republican tenets of consumption and manufacture. The panic's rash of bankruptcies and collapsing new institutions seemed to underscore the dire consequences of importing too many "superfluities" or too few necessities when appropriate regulatory safeguards were lacking. In fact, tariffs continued to rise.[14]

Thomas Cooper (1759–1839), a protégé of Jefferson, pro-French, and an advocate of slavery in his home state of South Carolina, stands as an example of protectionism's southern opponents. In terms reminiscent of the Calvinist injunction to a calling, Cooper praised the collective benefits of individual economic efforts, especially those centered on the internal craft trades and agriculture. A die-hard free-trade advocate, he urged readers to shed their oversolicitation of successful commercial interests whose credit originated abroad.

Recent work on southern economic thought reminds us that early national regions were not ideological monoliths. Some southerners, influenced by the work of Lord Shaftesbury, Francis Hutchinson, or Adam Smith, professed that natural sympathy curbed aggressive self-interest. The scenario imagined by Thomas Malthus taught others that government was not the proper vehicle for promoting private industry. And for some southern planters and publicists—including many wealthy slaveholders—free trade was but one part of a plan that eschewed agrarian simplicity, and they dreamed of a plantation system supported by internal improvements funded with federal and state aid and served by commerce. Although not modernizers in the same ways northern Whigs came to be, southern developers believed, by 1840, that a mixed economy held more promise than paeans to free trade.[15]

New thinking about credit and banking was a third topic that captured early national imaginations. Before the Revolution, political economists saw credit as a reflection of merchants' extant reputations. Building upon the Scottish Enlightenment's confidence in self-interest, and the years of currency finance and congressional funding, many began to view credit as an engine of change. By the time Hamilton's Bank of the United States (BUS) was in place, discussion about the dangers of a great institution tied to central government was distinct, in the minds of thousands of citizens, from the benefits of endless private negotiations that created enterprise based upon personal trust without an institutional "fund" of specie.[16] Scholars have retold many times how opinion divided sharply over the BUS. Advocates such as Oliver Wolcott of Connecticut imagined that banks would be of greatest benefit to an enterprising elite rather than middling inhabitants. Skeptics spoke from statehouses and pulpits attacking banks as reservoirs of aristocratic privilege that drew international traders into great debt with the lure of commercial credit. For some time scholarship has emphasized, too, how doubts about the efficacy of banks grew during the years of democratic rhetoric most closely associated with (although by no means the special preserve of) Jacksonians.[17] With the influence of labor radicals such as Langton Byllesby and Thomas Skidmore, who called for dissolving contemporary property relations and redistributing the wealth created by labor in more equitable proportions, there was little room for banks to extend credit to commercial farmers and ambitious artisans.[18]

But our historical perspective still lacks appreciation for what was surely a majority of Americans who swung to neither of these poles, who feared abuses of banks by particular economic interests but welcomed the credit of state and local banking when extended widely. Antifederalists in the 1780s, Democratic-Republicans in the 1790s, through moderate Whigs in the 1840s, pleaded not for the demise of banks but for their more controlled use for greater numbers of citizens. Prominent protectionists Daniel Raymond (1786–1849) and Hezekiah Niles expressed concerns by 1810 about the lack of capital funds to secure banks but never doubted their necessity. Raymond, Henry C. Carey (1793–1879), and Frederick List (1789–1846) held out the hope that by the 1830s bank credit might be distributed more widely. But Mathew Carey's earlier writings made the most impassioned appeal for compromise among banking interests. Carey advocated Federalist banking in the pages of his *American Museum* and served as a director of the Bank of Pennsylvania from 1802 to 1805, yet he also hoped state and national banks together would extend credit to needy commercial farmers, middling merchants, and manufacturing interests. Along with Albert Gallatin, William Crawford, and others— most of whom became Democratic-Republicans after 1794—Carey believed that the defeat of the BUS recharter movement in early 1811 signalled the unwise and illiberal views of the bank's opponents. It seemed inconceivable to him that the BUS could become a "monopoly" and that the nearly ninety state banks at that time could all cease to operate if the BUS continued. But BUS directors, charged Carey, were not blameless; he condemned their suspension of specie payments and discounts of state notes during the War of 1812, just when infant manufacturers needed extensive credit.[19]

The second Bank of the United States was chartered in 1816 and the number of state banks continued to grow, making extensive loans to a demanding public and funding them with specie borrowed from urban merchants. The desire for bank paper was so great, in fact, that few banks had protection against the flow of their notes into New England, where available specie was exported to pay commercial debts instead of supporting banknotes. As world prices for cotton fell after the war, as European economic revival slowed demand for American exports, and as some northern state banks failed, country banks in the West and Southeast foreclosed on myriad small investors. In mid-Atlantic states many internal improvements were simply abandoned as the country felt the shock of the Panic of 1819. Into the 1820s, structural economic problems also tended to fuel sectional differences; the continuing price slump for southern cotton, competition among northern manufacturers for protective tariffs to serve various particular interests, and scarcer bank credit in the Midwest for would-be developers and investors, all focussed attention on poorly integrated regions.

A fourth element of the public discussion about America's economic future involved internal improvements and manufactures. Eloquent historical explanations of the material "refinement" that muted the revolutionary generation's fears of luxury and self-interest, and that prompted new thinking about who entered and who left an emergent "middle class," have benefited by looking closely at this debate.[20] Among contemporary political economists and publicists was David Ricardo, whose *Principles of Political Economy* (1817) circulated widely and inspired advocates of manufactures, mechanics' banks, local canals, roads, and mill complexes to seek freedom from the "interfering hand" of government. Ricardo's defence of a producer ethic of free labor proved morally comforting to small investors in the American republic, for he sanctioned new enterprise on openly competitive terms by scorning both old corporate monopolies and new combinations of strikers and labor unionists. Few of these men-on-the-make rose to the heights of John Jacob Astor the far western fur trader, or Stephen Gerard with his empire of mining and canals; but great numbers of small manufacturers, inventors, shop owners, and grocers appropriated the image of self-made entrepreneurs.[21]

Most commentators, whether Federalist or Democratic-Republican, were more skeptical about Ricardo's message. Some writers noted that an entrepreneurial ethic excluded consideration of Americans who had little protection from the vagaries of early national markets: children and women moving into new work roles; squatters and shopkeepers filling the countryside; unlicensed peddlers and unemployed immigrants crowding city streets. Others proposed the need for extensive investments of public revenue—local, state, and federal—in mechanized enterprises that joined agricultural labor and "useful" manufactures. Jefferson's embargoes from 1807 to 1809 turned more attention from commerce toward roads, canals, bridges, improvement societies, and new agricultural techniques, many of which became utter failures, but which in their aggregate became a sign of the unleashed enthusiasm for taking risks with public funds. From 1789 to 1819 states issued over 2,500 special charters, while Congress outgrew many fears about the proposals that had appeared in Hamilton's 1791 *Report on Manufactures.*[22]

Henry Clay made one of the first systematic arguments for the benefits of domestic manufacturing as a supplement to the nation's commerce and agriculture under government guidance. In an address to Congress in 1810 that previewed his famous plan of 1824, Clay embraced an ambitious series of enterprises that would transform the nation from foreign commercial dependence to self-sufficiency. At the center of his vision—embraced by his newspaper publisher friend, Hezekiah Niles, and many manufacturers in the mid-Atlantic—was an expanding, energized people of middling, rising means who would rediscover the Protestant work ethic's injunctions to produce all manner of desirable goods and consume to levels of comfort but never to excess.[23]

Less influential in politics, but more innovative in economic thought, Carey, Raymond, John McVickar, Samuel Slater, and others, moved beyond Clay's insights and contemplated how value is created. They also offered new meanings for credit and posited the idea of national, as opposed to simply private, wealth in the domestic economy. In 1834 John Rae (1796–1872) broke new ground among American writers with a theory of capital formation that departed from both mercantile formulas based on capturing wealth from foreign nations and Smithian tenets of unleashed private accumulation. Rae proposed, instead, that the collective delayed gratification of wants throughout a producing population would create the savings for improvement and invention.[24] For his part, Raymond outlined a "national community" that emphasized collective economic interests, furthered by federal and state incentives. Although Raymond—and later Frederick List—was suspicious of the effects of factories and an extensive paper money supply, he insisted that governments could develop the home economy by dispensing with Smithian parsimony and spending more on public works, manufacturing technology, and incentives for consumption. Not savings, but high wages and spending would increase the "national product," free the country from the supremacy of foreign commerce, and improve the living standards of an emergent working class.[25] Into the next decade, Henry C. Carey discarded the gloom of Ricardo and Malthus and welcomed America's advance from a farming to an industrial nation. His was not so much a clarion call to redress the social cleavages developing across the nation, as it was a discourse on the potential for rising middling producers and consumers to see their capital and wages rise faster than the cost of living through intense entrepreneurial effort and America's natural bounty.[26]

Carey's optimistic forecasts did not reflect the actual pathway of economic development in the years before the Panic of 1837.[27] Customary expectations of household production and consumption persisted at many millsites and small enterprises, even as they were transformed by increasing division of labor, concentrations of capital, and separation of ownership from rural and urban wage labor. Most of the nearly eighty textile mills in New England and the mid-Atlantic were small operations and did not survive the Panic of 1819, but a few became consolidated enterprises. Brickmaking and sawmilling sprang up throughout the countryside, and small textile mills and machine tool shops dotted the near West. New rural-trading-milling towns emerged to link the hinterlands with port cities. Flour milling in Wilmington, for example, grew up both naturally and by the aggressive design of entrepreneurs who saw the potential to connect one of America's wheat belts to Philadelphia and foreign markets. Merchant mills replaced rural mills in areas devoted to the export trades, and square-rigged vessels complemented the carrying trade of sloops in a dozen cities. The early China trade, the Erie Canal, and the Boston Manufacturing Company were spectacular sponges for urban and migrant labor in their time, but capital for manufacturing was still in few hands, and down to at least 1827 employment in cities proved more temporary than secure, while tenancy and migration rose. A cash-based economy had become acceptable to large numbers of producers and consumers before there were sufficient market linkages to make and move the goods that money could buy. Higher levels of consumption began to alter gender and class relations before Americans understood changing forms of production and capital formation, and before they glimpsed the home market.[28]

The ambiguities and partial successes of these unprecedented efforts to transform the American economy in the early republic had their parallel in the writings of political economists. The rhetoric of hope in their treatises consistently ran ahead of Americans' half-steps of understanding about periodic downturns and their shortages of capital for the new enterprises they imagined. We would do well to study the ways that Americans understood their economy, as we continue to explore what they actually accomplished. We know very little about how Americans rethought their understanding of commerce as a rapidly expanding people improved the countryside and shifted their demand for resources. Who were the boosters and funders of local experiments with field rotations, hybrid animals and plants, new kinds of outbuildings, dairy product marketing, and ubiquitous textiles production? Newspapers, almanacs, and advice manuals invited Americans to make their nation a consuming democracy but we are largely ignorant about the discrete decisions people made about what, and how much, to produce for family necessity or market to distant ports. Although we have shed the myth of rural self-sufficiency, we have not yet examined the extent to which rural families may have shared certain characteristics of the self-employed urban craftsman or shopkeeper, and whether they shared a free labor ideology or producer ethic across geographic divisions. Did the gap grow larger between a small-producer ideal of independence and the reality of market, landlord, and debt dependencies; or was the burden of reality great enough to shatter intellectual dreams of personal independence? We still know as little about the presence of wage and cash relations in the countryside as we know about the presence of neighborhood marketing, gardening, and producing for household consumption in the cities before the 1830s.[29]

The search for characteristics of the "middling sort" has proved especially elusive, in part because traditional occupations and status categories fragmented as the pace of industrialization quickened by the 1830s, and in part because a malleable entrepreneurial ethos subsumed many distinctive identities. Ironically, economic interests were dividing along class, regional, and sectional lines just at the moment that Raymond and Rae began to conceptualize a national market characterized by its opportunities for a growing middle strata. But were entrepreneurial artisans, small planters, commercial farmers, urban professionals, manufacturers, merchants, and wealthy artisans all striving together to reach an imagined pinnacle of wealth? Or, did a significant portion of them choose economic security, a degree of comfort at a low level of risk, savings over investment, diversification of their enterprises over economies of scale and specialization? Did moral intonation fade or grow, and did Americans continue to approve of government intervention—albeit on new terms—even as individualism became a hallmark of the era? A clearer portrait of this variegated "middle" will need to include more about local and regional mobilization of capital, county and state government involvement, conflicts over goals and consequences of improvement, and the demands of transforming successive stages of the frontier. As the work is undertaken, it will serve us well to rediscover the discussions Americans had about who should direct, and who should benefit from, economic change, discussions that embodied many creative ambiguities and persisted well beyond the early national years.

NOTES

1. Writers since at least Sir James Stewart had deployed the term "political economy" with reference not only to the joining of economic policy making and national/imperial security, but also with reference to the activities of individuals in civil society; see, for example, Frank A. Fetter, "The Early History of Political Economy in the United States," *Proceedings of the American Philosophical Society*, 87 (July 1943); Hiram Caton, "The Pre-Industrial Economics of Adam Smith," *Journal of Economic History* 45 (Dec. 1985), 833–53; C. B. Macpherson, ed., *Political Economy and Political Theory* (Toronto, 1974); and Paul Conkin, *Prophets of Prosperity: America's First Political Economists* (Bloomington, 1980). For ideas in this and the next paragraph, see especially Gordon S. Wood, *The Radicalism of the American Revolution* (New York, 1992); Marc Egnal and Joseph Ernst, "An Economic Interpretation of the American Revolution," *William and Mary Quarterly*, 29 (Jan. 1972), 3–36; Curtis P. Nettels, *The Emergence of a National Economy, 1775–1815* (New York, 1962); John J. McCusker and Russell R. Menard, *The Economy of British America, 1607–1789* (Chapel Hill, 1985); Ronald Hoffman *et al.*, eds., *The Economy of Early America: The*

Revolutionary Period, 1763–1790, (Charlottesville, 1988); Jackson Turner Main, *The Sovereign States, 1775–1783* (New York, 1973); and Cathy Matson and Peter S. Onuf, "Toward a Republican Empire: Interest and Ideology in Revolutionary America," *American Quarterly,* 37 (Fall 1985), 496–531. There has been no study to replace the magisterial work of Joseph Dorfman, *The Economic Mind in American Civilization* (5 vols., New York, 1946–1959).

2. On the economy of the 1780s, see especially Drew R. McCoy, *The Elusive Republic: Political Economy in Jeffersonian America* (Chapel Hill, 1980); and John R. Nelson, Jr., *Liberty and Property: Political Economy and Policymaking in the New Nation, 1789–1812* (Baltimore, 1987).

3. Work on debtor rebellions has been an important part of early national political economy. See, for example, David P. Szatmary, *Shays' Rebellion: The Making of an Agrarian Insurrection* (Amherst, 1980); and Richard D. Brown, "Shays's Rebellion and the Ratification of the Constitution in Massachusetts," in Richard Beeman, Stephen Botein, and Edward C. Carter II, eds., *Beyond Confederation: Origins of the Constitution and American National Identity* (Chapel Hill, 1987), 113–27. On state experiments, Cathy D. Matson and Peter S. Onuf, *A Union of Interests: Political and Economic Thought in Revolutionary America* (Lawrence, 1990), chap. 4.

4. On economic aspects of the Constitution, see, for example, E. James Ferguson, "Political Economy, Public Liberty, and the Formation of the Constitution," *William and Mary Quarterly,* 40 (July 1983), 389–412; Gordon C. Bjork, "The Weaning of the American Economy: Independence, Market Changes, and Economic Development," *Journal of Economic History,* 24 (Dec. 1964), 541–60; and Jennifer Nedelsky, *Private Property and the Limits of American Constitutionalism: The Madisonian Framework and Its Legacy* (Chicago, 1990).

5. For a recent contribution along these lines, see Christopher L. Tomlins, *Law, Labor, and Ideology in the Early American Republic* (Cambridge, 1993).

6. Tench Coxe, "Sketches of the Subject of American Manufactures" (1787), in Coxe, *A View of the United States of America* (Philadelphia, 1794), 54; Coxe, "Statements . . . in Reply to the Assertions and Predictions of Lord Sheffield" (1791), *ibid.,* 260; [Hezekiah Niles], *Niles' Weekly Register* (Baltimore), 6 (1814), 395. For historians' views about land and markets, Robert D. Mitchell, *Commercialism and Frontier: Perspectives on the Early Shennandoah Valley* (Charlottesville, 1977); Wood, *Radicalism of the American Revolution,* chap. 17; Joyce Appleby, "Commercial Farming and the 'Agrarian Myth' in the Early Republic," *Journal of American History,* 68 (March 1982), 833–49; Matson and Onuf, *Union of Interests,* chap. 8; Paul G. E. Clemens and Lucy Simler, "Rural Labor and the Farm Household in Chester County, Pa, 1750–1820," in Stephen Innes, ed., *Work and Labor in*

Early America (Chapel Hill, 1988), 106–43; Stuart Bruchey, ed., *Cotton and the Growth of the American Economy, 1790–1860: Sources and Readings* (New York, 1967); and Robert Gallman, "The Agricultural Sector and the Pace of Economic Growth: U.S. Experience in the Nineteenth Century," in David C. Klingman and Richard K. Vedder, eds., *Essays in Nineteenth Century Economic History: The Old Northwest* (Athens, OH, 1975), 35–76.

7. [James Madison], "Fashion," *National Gazette*, March 20, 1792; Madison to N. P. Trist, Jan. 26, 1828, in James Madison, *The Writings of James Madison*, ed. Gaillard Hunt (9 vols., New York, 1900–1910), IX, 304–05. The best work on population for the era is Peter D. McClelland and Richard J. Zeckhauser, *Demographic Dimensions of the New Republic: American Interregional Migration, Vital Statistics, and Manumissions, 1800–1860* (New York, 1982).

8. On embargoes, see Merrill D. Peterson, "Thomas Jefferson and Commercial Policy, 1783–1793," *William and Mary Quarterly*, 31 (Oct. 1974), 633–46; and Burton Spivak, *Jefferson's English Crisis: Commerce, Embargo, and the Republican Revolution* (Charlottesville, 1979).

9. For the persistence of the family farm and strategies not necessarily related to profit making, see, for example, Jeremy Atack and Fred Bateman, *To Their Own Soil: Agriculture in the Antebellum North* (Ames, 1987); Percy W. Bidwell, "The Rural Economy in New England at the Beginning of the Nineteenth Century," Connecticut Academy of Arts and Sciences, *Transactions*, 20 (New Haven, 1916), 241–399. For full citations on the literature of the transition to capitalism see note 4 in Paul A. Gilje, "The Rise of Capitalism in the Early Republic," in this volume.

10. Mathew Carey, *Address to the Wealthy of the Land, Ladies as Well as Gentlemen, on the Character, Conduct, Situation, and Prospects, of those Whose Sole Dependence for Subsistence, is on the Labour of their Hands* (Philadelphia, 1831), esp. 2–9. For effects of the Napoleonic Wars, see Steven J. Watts, *The Republic Reborn: War and the Making of Liberal America, 1790–1820* (Baltimore, 1987). On Carey, see especially Kenneth Wyer Rowe, *Mathew Carey, A Study in American Economic Development* (Baltimore, 1933).

11. John McVickar, *Outlines of Political Economy* (New York, 1825).

12. George S. Hillard, *The Dangers and Duties of the Mercantile Profession* (Boston, 1850), 45, 16, 13.

13. Mathew Carey, *The Olive Branch: or, Faults on Both Sides, Federal and Democratic* (Philadelphia, 1814) sold over 10,000 copies and attempted to reconcile the differences between Democratic-Republicans and Federalists. On Malthus, see especially James Russell Gibson, Jr., *Americans versus Malthus: The Population Debate in the Early Republic, 1790–1840* (New York, 1989). Ideas in this paragraph are related closely to writings about the labor theory of value. Present in Locke's writings as the simple notion

that wealth came not from circulation of goods and balance of trade, but from the labor of myriad individuals, the theory was given new twists of meaning by 1800, some of them introduced by Ricardo. All writings agreed that wealth was created by human effort and represented the collective of wants and needs in a population. From there, however, theorists diverged. Some held that it entailed a bundle of rights and responsibilities; some countered that it was free association modified by degrees of government protection. Some used the labor theory of value to criticize those who did not work with their hands; others deployed it to defend unequal property. A small group of policy-makers wrote about the "labor" of bankers, landlords, and land speculators, thereby using a venerable set of tenets to ensconce emerging property arrangements in an increasingly unequal society. Helpful starting points include Sean Wilentz, *Chants Democratic: New York City & Rise of the American Working Class, 1788–1850* (New York, 1984); and Howard B. Rock, *Artisans of the New Republic: The Tradesmen of New York City in the Age of Jefferson* (New York, 1979).

14. Whether artisans' arguments for tariffs were derived from a republican heritage, or from the newer language of democracy, entrepreneurship, and self-interest, is unsettled in historians' dialogues. For the former, see, for example, Charles Steffen, "Changes in the Organization of Artisan Production in Baltimore, 1790–1820," *William and Mary Quarterly*, 36 (Jan. 1979), 101–17; and Wilentz, *Chants Democratic*, 1–103; for the latter, see, for example, Joyce Appleby, *Capitalism and a New Social Order: The Republican Vision of the 1790s* (New York, 1984); and Eric Foner, *Tom Paine and Revolutionary America* (New York, 1976). For further literature on artisans in this period see notes 17 and 18 in Gilje, "The Rise of Capitalism," in this volume. On business aspects of tariffs and the panic, the best study is still Murray N. Rothbard, *The Panic of 1819: Reactions and Policies* (New York, 1962); see also, Thomas C. Cochran, "The Business Revolution," *American Historical Review*, 79 (Dec. 1974), 1449–66; Nathan Miller, *The Enterprise of a Free People: Aspects of Economic Development in New York Sate during the Canal Period, 1792–1838* (Ithaca, 1962); and Samuel Rezneck, "The Depression of 1819–1822: A Social History," *American Historical Review*, 39 (Oct. 1933), 28–47.

15. Thomas Cooper, *Lectures on the Elements of Political Economy*, (1829; 2d ed., Columbia, SC, 1830). Francis Wayland (1796–1865) fused Baptist theology and free trade. On southern agrarians generally, Joseph J. Persky, *The Burden of Dependency: Colonial Themes in Southern Economic Thought* (Baltimore, 1992); and Joyce E. Chaplin, *An Anxious Pursuit: Agricultural Innovation and Modernity in the Lower South, 1730–1815* (Chapel Hill, 1993). For a reassessment of the agrarian bent of southern writers, see Vicki

Vaughn Johnson, *The Men and the Vision of the Southern Commercial Convention, 1845–1871* (Columbia, MO, 1992).

16. A valuable summary of these connections is Janet A. Riesman, "Republican Revisions: Political Economy in New York after the Panic of 1819," in William Pencak and Conrad E. Wright, eds., *New York and the Rise of American Capitalism; Economic Development and the Social Political and History of an American State, 1780–1870* (New York, 1989), 1–44.

17. Edward Carter II, "The Birth of A Political Economist: Mathew Carey and the Recharter Fight of 1810–1811," *Pennsylvania History*, 33 (July 1966), 274–88. For opposition to rechartering the Bank of the United States see especially Marvin Meyers, *The Jacksonian Persuasion: Politics and Belief* (Stanford, 1957), chaps. 5, 6.

18. See, for example, Langton Byllesby, *Observations of the Sources and Effects of Unequal Wealth* (New York, 1826); and Thomas Skidmore, *The Rights of Man to Property* (New York, 1829). Being hired and fired at will, and deskilled over time, laboring Americans already knew something about supply and demand; their response was to discuss the dignity of labor, the ancient beliefs in justice, equity, fair wages and prices, even as they pursued personal opportunities.

19. Carter, "The Birth of a Political Economist," 274–88; Daniel Raymond, *Thoughts on Political Economy* (Baltimore, 1820); Henry C. Carey, *Principles of Political Economy* (3 vols., Philadelphia, 1837–1840); Friederick List, *Outlines of American Political Economy* (Philadelphia, 1827), which was a refutation of Cooper; and List, *National System of Political Economy*, trans. Stephen Colwell (1841; rep., Philadelphia, 1856), which emphasized the productive potential of a regulated economy.

20. Richard L. Bushman, *The Refinement of America: Persons, Houses, Cities* (New York, 1992); Wood, *Radicalism of the American Revolution*; and Stuart Blumin, *The Emergence of the Middle Class: Social Experience in the American City, 1760–1900* (Cambridge, 1989). These works often coincide with concerns about the "market revolution"; see, for example, Charles G. Sellers, *The Market Revolution, Jacksonian America, 1815–1846* (New York, 1991); and Michael A. Bernstein and Sean Wilentz, "Marketing, Commerce and Capitalism in Rural Massachusetts," *Journal of Economic History*, 44 (March 1984), 171–73.

21. Conkin, *Prophets of Prosperity*, chap. 5; Lee Soltow, "Economic Inequality in the United States in the Period from 1790 to 1860," *Journal of Economic History*, 31 (Dec. 1971), 822–39; James P. Ronda, *Astoria and Empire* (Lincoln, 1990).

22. See different perspectives in Tench Coxe, Hugh Williamson, William Vans Murray, Richard Price, and Timothy Dwight. On manufacturing, see John R. Nelson, Jr., "Alexander Hamilton and American Manufac-

turing: A Reexamination," *Journal of American History*, 65 (March 1979), 971–95; Jacob E. Cooke, "Tench Coxe, Alexander Hamilton, and the Encouragement of American Manufactures," *William and Mary Quarterly*, 32 (July 1975), 369–92; John E. Sawyer, "The Social Basis of the American System of Manufactures," *Journal of Economic History*, 14 (Fall 1954), 361–79; Samuel Rezneck, "The Rise and Early Development of Industrial Consciousness in the United States, 1760–1830," *Journal of Economic and Business History*, 4 (Aug. 1932), 784–811; Michael Brewster Folsom and Steven D. Lubar, *The Philosophy of Manufactures: Early Debates over Industrialization in the United States* (Cambridge, MA, 1982); and Carl Siracusa, *A Mechanical People: Perceptions of the Industrial order in Massachusetts, 1815–1880* (Middletown, 1979). For internal improvements, see Carter Goodrich, "Internal Improvements Reconsidered," *Journal of Economic History*, 30 (June 1970), 289–311; Christopher Baer, *The Canals and Railroads of the Mid-Atlantic States, 1800–1860* (Wilmington, 1981); Peter Way, *Common Labour: Workers and the Digging of North American Canals, 1780–1860* (New York, 1993); and John Lauritz Larson, "A Bridge, A Dam, A River: Liberty and Innovation in the Early Republic," *Journal of the Early Republic*, 7 (Winter 1987), 351–75.

23. *Niles' Weekly Register* was published in Baltimore from 1811 to 1818; see also, Richard Stone, *Hezekiah Niles as an Economist* (Baltimore, 1933). For Clay's political economy, the best short account is in Daniel Walker Howe, *The Political Culture of the American Whigs* (Chicago, 1979), chap. 6.

24. John Rae, *Statement of Some New Principles on the Subject of Political Economy* (Boston, 1834), which was written to refute free trade and Smithian tenets. He also analyzed the costs of production and reproduction in his "activist" economy, both of which were novel at the time.

25. Raymond, *Thoughts on Political Economy;* List, *Outlines of American Political Economy;* List, *National System of Political Economy.*

26. Henry C. Carey, *Essay on the Rate of Wages: With an Examination of the Causes of the Differences in the Condition of the Labouring Population Throughout the World* (Philadelphia, 1835); Carey, *Principles of Political Economy.* For the renewed economic downturn, see, for example, Peter Temin, *The Jacksonian Economy* (New York, 1969); and Samuel Rezneck, "The Social History of an American Depression, 1837–1843," *American Historical Review*, 40 (July 1935), 662–87.

27. To be sure, many fears about fast-paced change, government intervention in the economy, or sudden transformation of "natural" social relations into "artificial" dependencies, debt, and material accumulation, lingered. John Adams, for example, lamented the demise of economic and social distinctions that were immersed in the sea of moral neutrality

and excessive competition. John Taylor of Caroline was equally scornful of the new economic values, but from the agrarian, southern standpoint, and looked with horror upon Hamiltonian institutions and the commercial avarice of the Napoleonic Wars. Nostalgic, yet no defender of the planter elite, Taylor was a favorite of dissenting Republicans and then Democrats long after his death in 1824. See Conkin, *Prophets of Prosperity*, chap. 1.

28. On the transition, see Allan Kulikoff, "The Transition to Capitalism in Rural America," *William and Mary Quarterly*, 46 (Jan. 1989), 120–44. Although the terms "capital" and "capitalist" had become familiar to many Americans before the end of the eighteenth century, thinking about "capitalism" or a national market and labor relations dependent upon the extraction of surplus value came later. For developments mentioned in this paragraph, see Cathy Matson, "The Revolution, The Constitution, and the New Nation," in Stanley Engerman and Robert Gallman, eds., *The Cambridge Economic History of the United States*, Vol. I, *The Colonial Era* (Cambridge, 1996), 363–401. Much valuable information is still to be found in George Rogers Taylor, *The Transportation Revolution, 1815–1860* (New York, 1951).

29. In addition to the items cited in this note see notes 4, 19, and 22 in Gilje, "The Rise of Capitalism," in this volume. Sarah McMahon, "Laying Foods By: Gender, Dietary Decisions, and the Technology of Food Preservation in New England Households, 1750–1850," in Judith A. McGaw, ed., *Early American Technology: Making and Doing Things From the Colonial Era to 1850* (Chapel Hill, 1994), 164–96; Jack Larkin, "Labor is the Great Thing in Farming: The Farm Laborers of the Ward Family of Shrewsbury, Massachusetts, 1787–1860," *Proceedings of the American Antiquarian Society*, 99 (April 1989), 189–226; Donald Parkerson, "Agriculture and the Cult of Mobility: The Economic Transformation of Rural New York in the Mid-Nineteenth Century" (Ph.D. diss., University of Illinois, Chicago, 1983); Margaret Martin, *Merchants and the Trade of the Connecticut River Valley, 1750–1820* (Northampton, MA, 1938–1939); Charles Hammond, "Where the Arts and the Virtues Meet: Country Life Near Boston, 1637–1864," (Ph.D. diss., Boston University, 1982); and David G. Hackett, *The Rude Hand of Innovation: Religion and Social Order in Albany, New York, 1652–1836* (New York, 1991).

EIGHT

The Enemy is Us: Democratic Capitalism in the Early Republic

GORDON S. WOOD

OF ALL THE "ISMS" THAT AFFLICT US, capitalism is the worst. According to many scholars, capitalism has been ultimately responsible for much of what ails us, both in the past and in the present, including our race problem, our grossly unequal distribution of wealth, and the general sense of malaise and oppression that academics in particular feel. It is not surprising therefore that scholars should be interested in the origins of such a powerful force, especially one that seems to affect them so personally.

The trouble is we scholars cannot agree on the nature of the beast. Some identify it with a general market economy; others, following Marx, with a particular mode of production, involving a bourgeoisie that owns the means of production and a proletariat that is forced to sell its labor for monetary wages; still others, following Weber, with a system of calculative and secularized rationalism; and still others, with simple hard work and a spirit of development. As has often been pointed out, the way in which scholars define the term "capitalism" usually determines the results of their analysis.[1]

The confusion has gotten so great that we now have competing and contradictory studies that show that the first two centuries of early American history were either capitalist from the beginning or never capitalist at all. Stephen Innes has recently argued that the seventeenth-century New England Puritans were "bearers of a culture that was already capitalist when they arrived in the New World."[2] At the same time Michael Merrill has contended that the early nineteenth-century American economy, despite the presence of widespread market exchanges, private property, wage labor, and sophisticated financial instruments, was not yet capitalist. Regardless of their differences, however, both historians share a common aversion to out-and-out possessive individualism and want to show us that in America's past there did exist versions of capitalism, or at least a commercial market economy, that had a human face.[3]

Actually these two seemingly polar positions represent the extremes of a debate historians have been having over the nature of early New England's society and economy, the place where presumably modern American capitalism first arose.[4] From almost the beginning of professional historical scholarship most American historians assumed that nearly all early American farmers, including those in New England, were incipient capitalists, eager to make money and get land and get ahead. Most farmers, it seemed, were involved in trade of various sorts—sending tobacco and wheat to England and Europe, selling fish, foodstuffs, and lumber to the West Indies, and exchanging a wide variety of goods among themselves. For these historians, usually labeled "liberal" or "market" historians these days, explaining the origins of capitalism in America has never been an issue: America has always been capitalistic.

A quarter century or so ago a group of historians, generally labeled "social" or "moral economy" historians, began challenging this view of early America as a modern market-oriented capitalistic world. The colonial farmers, particularly the New England farmers, it seems, did not possess a capitalistic mentality after all; they were not primarily interested in working for profit—a lack of interest in the bottom line that for these historians is something to be cherished. The less capitalism the better, as far as they are concerned.

This "transition to capitalism" debate has gone on now for several decades, and as a consequence we certainly know much more about the behavior and values of the early New England farmers than we did before. Especially helpful in the debate has been the work of Winifred Barr Rothenberg. In *From Market-Places to a Market Economy* Rothenberg has cleared the air of a lot of cant by simply concentrating on some basic questions about the rural New England economy that can be empirically verified. By analyzing the behavior of the prices of farm commodities, farm labor, and rural savings, she has been able to date the emergence of a market economy in the New England countryside, placing it in the last two decades of the eighteenth century following the American Revolution.[5]

Although Rothenberg saw herself writing in opposition to the "moral economy" historians, whom she affectionately calls her "dear enemies," her work actually has helped to reconcile the differences between these "dear enemies" and most market historians, including herself.[6] Backed by the impressive empirical investigations of Rothenberg, scholars now seem to have attained a remarkable amount of agreement over the behavior of people in early America, even if they cannot agree on what to call that behavior. Although most are doubtful that capitalism came over on the first ships, they realize that commercial activities in the New World were present from the beginning. Although historians recognize that a new stage in America's commercial development was reached in the middle of the eighteenth century, many seem to agree that it was the American Revolution above all that gave birth to something that can be called capitalism. In fact, writes Allan Kulikoff, a neo-Marxist who has tried to mediate the debate, "the American Revolution may have been the most crucial event in the creation of capitalism."[7] James Henretta, probably the most influential of the moral economy historians, cites Rothenberg's findings in support of his thesis "that the emergence of a new system of economic behavior, values, and institutions occurred at the beginning of the nineteenth century."[8] Moreover, both the market and the moral economy historians agree that New England farmers engaged in local exchanges throughout the eighteenth century. If these local exchanges could be seen as variants of market behavior, then the differences between the two groups of historians would tend to collapse. In fact, Kulikoff admits as much when he says that "the two sides contend over the *degree* of local self-sufficiency and the *extent* of market exchange rather than the *fact* of exchange."[9]

The problem seems to be the moral economy historians' commitment to Marx's distinction between producing for use and producing for exchange, a distinction that in fact seems very dubious. When the social or moral economy historians come to examine the actual behavior of the New England farmers, they keep falling back on this distinction to explain why the farmers were not really market-oriented—in effect relying on their ability to decipher the motives of these rural folk. Thus when farmers locally exchanged wheat for tools or vegetables for cloth, "their goal," says Henretta, "was not profit but the acquisition of a needed item for use." Even when farmers sold some of their goods to the wider market outside of their region, "their chief purpose," writes Christopher Clark, "was not to engage in the market economy but to satisfy the demands placed on them by the household economy." What seems to be the farmers' profit-seeking or land speculation the moral economy historians dismiss as merely the farmers' looking after the needs of their families. No matter how sharp or avaricious the farmers might be—and even the moral economy historians admit that they could indeed be sharp and avaricious—these characteristics apparently did not turn them into entrepreneurs; as Henretta says, "there was no determined pursuit of profit."[10]

These moral economy historians seem to have an overdrawn and caricatured image of an entrepreneur or capitalist as someone who thinks about nothing but the bottom line and has an all-consuming drive for profits that rides roughshod over the needs of his family or his relationship with the community. If this is what it takes, then very few farmers in history have ever been this kind of selfish, profit-maximizing individualist.[11]

It is these historians' deep aversion to capitalism that lies behind their caricatured images of capitalists. This aversion requires evil-intentioned individuals; it is no easy matter morally condemning people who are well-intentioned and have no sense of the bad and exploitative consequences of their actions. Perhaps it is this problem of assigning moral responsibility for the effects of capitalism that accounts for these social historians' lingering commitment to Marxism: Marxist theory allows for moral condemnation but in a scientific mode. "Marxists," writes Kulikoff (who sees himself as someone "influenced by Marx and Marxist writings"), "understand capitalism as a mode of production in which capitalists, who own the means of production, expropriate surplus value from proletarians, who own only their labor power." The problem with this traditional Marxist definition, as Kulikoff admits, is that it does not fit rural American conditions. Most American farmers in the North, especially in New England, were small producers who used family labor and only occasionally employed outsiders; thus they were "neither exploiter nor exploited," but both at the same time.[12]

The neo-Marxist historian Michael Merrill escapes from this Marxist conundrum by denying that this small producer economy of New England, however dominated by market exchanges, was ever capitalist. Kulikoff, however, admits the presence of capitalism and consequently ties himself in knots trying to fit the circumstances of rural New England into orthodox Marxian theory. He proposes that we consider farmers as resembling both proletarians and bourgeoisie and thereby locate them in more than one class simultaneously. "The idea of contradictory class locations," he believes, "suggests a way to understand American farmers." So it goes with "class," "expropriation," "surplus value," "proletarianization," and all the other special terms that Marxist historians of early rural America have to fit together and relate to a contradictory reality. One would think that such awkward convolutions would sooner or later lead these historians to wonder about the usefulness of their Marxian theory.[13]

No doubt it would help if we got rid of the term "capitalism" altogether. After all, it was not until the early twentieth century that the word acquired its modern usage.[14] But this is no longer possible. The term is already too much a part of our culture and scholarly discourse to be ignored. Although many historians seldom use it in anything but an unfriendly manner, we will have to get along with it as best we can and just try to make clear what we mean when we do use it.

Merrill has tried to do just that. Realizing that the long-standing identification of capitalism with commercial enterprise and a general market economy is disastrous for any moral condemnation of capitalism (there being these days, it seems, no alternative to markets), Merrill has sought to redefine capitalism as just one particular market economy among many. "Capitalism, properly speaking," he says, "is not just an economic system based on market exchange, private property, wage labor, and sophisticated financial instruments." These are necessary but not sufficient features. "Capitalism, more precisely, is a market economy ruled by, or in the interests of, capitalists." In other words, capitalism involves politics, power, and the exploitation of one class by another, in particular, in the early republic the exploitation of the farmers, artisans, and laborers by those whom Merrill calls "the monied classes." Since in the decades following the Revolution the American economy, however market-oriented and intensely commercialized it may have been, seemed to remain under the control of small producers and not the so-called capitalistic moneyed classes, Merrrill can make his astonishing claim that the American Revolution was "a profoundly anticapitalist enterprise." The burgeoning and prosperous economy of the early republic, far from representing "an emergent, radically new, capitalist order," was, Merrill says, in reality only "the expansion of a dynamic, profoundly anticapitalist, and democratic old order."[15]

This is an unconventional argument, to say the least, and it seems unlikely that it will take hold: it runs too much against the grain of our traditional identification of early nineteenth-century capitalism with a free enterprise market economy, an identification shared by nearly all the "transition-to-capitalism" historians. But it does have the merit of helping us to define more precisely what we mean by capitalism in the early republic. Merrill suggests that his small producer class includes not only most farmers and laborers but most artisans as well. Against these democratic anticapitalists he places the capitalists, or "the monied classes," composed of "merchants, financiers, or budding master manufacturers,"[16] The problem arises with this last group, the "budding master manufacturers." We today might readily agree that these master manufacturers (soon to be labeled businessmen) are capitalists or future capitalists, but in the eighteenth century should they be separated from the rest of the artisans? Contemporaries in the early republic, including the master manufacturers themselves, did not think so. They still thought of these master manufacturers, however wealthy, as men who worked for a living with their hands, and thus they grouped them with the other laborers in the society. The Providence Association of Mechanics and Manufacturers organized in 1789 was composed of men who ranged from among the wealthiest property-holders in the city to the poorest. All, however, were still regarded as workingmen.[17]

The issue for the society of the early republic was not who was a capitalist, but rather who was a laborer. As John Adams put it in 1790, "the great question will forever remain, *who shall work?*"[18] Gentlemen presumably did not work, but everyone else did, especially artisans. The status of artisans or mechanics, because it was changing rapidly, is a problem for us. We seem to agree that artisans represented a variety of people and ranks, ranging from very wealthy to poor, with most being thought to occupy the middling ranks in the society. In the eighteenth century artisans were usually organized vertically by craft. That is, each craft—whether silversmiths, shoemakers, coopers, or whatever—was organized into three gradations—masters, journeymen, and apprentices—and in the eighteenth century these vertical gradations within each craft tended to identify with each other and their particular craft rather than horizontally with the masters, journeymen, or apprentices in other crafts.[19]

In the eighteenth century most aristocrats or gentlemen who did not have to work with their hands still lumped together into the ignoble and mean category of "laborers" all these varieties of craftsmen and gradations of artisans and mechanics, mingling together in their minds wealthy masters with the lowliest and poorest of workers.[20] Despite a growing appreciation of the value of labor and heightened egalitarian sentiments, many eighteenth-century gentry, in other words, still clung to the two-thousand-year-old prejudice against manual labor, a prejudice that made it very difficult for artisans or mechanics, however rich and respectable, to claim genteel status as long as they continued to work for a living with their hands, or even to run a business that involved employees working with their hands. This is why Franklin made so much of his retirement from his printing business at the age of 42: only then could he become a full-fledged gentleman and devote himself to science and public service.[21]

This contempt was real and in the 1790s was still felt by all "laborers," even those who differed from each other as greatly as Walter Brewster, a young struggling shoemaker of Canterbury, Connecticut, did from Christopher Leffingwell, a well-to-do manufacturer of Norwich, Connecticut, who owned several mills and shops and was his town's largest employer. Given their common consciousness of themselves as mean "laborers" having to work for a living, men like Brewster and Leffingwell naturally allied in political movements on behalf of artisans and understandably sought to identify their "laboring interest" with "the general or common interest" of the whole state. We historians are often puzzled by such seemingly incongruous alliances and apparently irrational feelings of identity among manufacturers who differed so dramatically in their wealth and scale of activity: but this puzzlement comes from our anticipating the future too quickly.[22]

In time, of course, the once-vertically organized artisans would split apart horizontally, separating into rich master-businessmen (or employers) and poor journeymen- and apprentice-workers (or employees). But this important development would come haltingly and confusedly, and we distort our understanding of the eighteenth century if we anachronistically rush it.[23] In the early decades of the republic large-scale manufacturers like Leffingwell and small craftsmen like Brewster still shared a common resentment of a genteel world that had humiliated them and scorned their "laboring" status from the beginning of time. Despite their obvious differences, socially and psychologically these workers and future businessmen were still the same. In 1792 the diverse members of the Providence Association of Mechanics and Manufacturers, for example, celebrated their common interest as workers, "instead of repining that Providence has not destined us, to move in a higher Sphere."[24] In the late eighteenth century both proto-employers and proto-employees were included, and included themselves, in the category of those who had to work for a living, an identification that has caused no end of trouble for modern historians looking to celebrate a heroic working class but despising businessmen.

Perhaps we can help to clarify our understanding of what was happening by focusing on William Manning, the self-educated common New England farmer whose writings Michael Merrill and Sean Wilentz have recently edited.[25] Indeed, figuring out where to place people like Manning in the society may be a way of making sense of the transition to capitalism in the early republic.

Manning, writing under the name of a "Laborer," realized only too keenly that for ages leisured aristocrats had held workers like him in contempt. Therefore, in response to the traditional view of work as demeaning and contemptible, he offered a vigorous defense of labor as the source of property and productivity in the society. As vivid as Manning's writings were, however, they were not unusual: attacks on the leisured aristocratic few and defenses of labor by mechanics, farmers, and other laborers like Manning became increasingly common in postrevolutionary America.[26] Indeed, the Americans' celebration of work in these years was far more successful in conquering the culture, at least in the northern states, than comparable efforts in Europe. By the early decades of the nineteenth century there were very few gentry left in the northern states of America who could openly admit that they did not work for a living, in other words, who could openly admit any longer that they were fundamentally different from the likes of William Manning, Walter Brewster, or Christopher Leffingwell. We are only beginning to appreciate the historical character of work and the way its changing meanings at the end of the eighteenth century contributed to the development of capitalism.[27]

Manning, writing in the 1790s, of course, had no idea that he was participating in the cause of capitalism. All he could see was a great social struggle in which "the whole contention lies between those that labor for a living and those that do not." In Manning's opinion those who did not have to work were mainly big merchants, professionals, executive and judicial officers of government, "and all the rich who could live on their incomes without bodily labor." They were the kinds of men who had a "sense of superiority" and who "generally associate together and look down with too much contempt on those that labor." Although Manning at times included stock-jobbers and speculators within his category of the leisured, he was scarcely thinking of those who did not labor for a living as "capitalists." Rather his leisured few, numbering about one-eighth of the population, were those traditionally referred to as aristocrats or gentlemen. Most such gentlemen did not work for a living, in any traditional meaning of the term, or if they did, they worked solely with their heads. Instead, as Manning (if not his editors) realized, the incomes of such leisured gentry "lie chiefly in money at interest, rents, salaries, and fees that are fixed on the nominal value of money," which is why these gentry were generally opposed to paper money and its inflationary effects.[28]

Although we might want anachronistically to designate as capitalists some of Manning's leisured few, those Federalist leaders (and they were essentially whom Manning meant by his few who did not labor for a living) were not really the persons most responsible for the emergence of the dynamic capitalistic economy of the early republic.[29] We make a big mistake thinking that capitalism was created mainly by Alexander Hamilton and a few stockjobbers, speculators, and wealthy merchants. If any group was most responsible for the burgeoning capitalist economy of the early republic, it was the Republicans and all the commercially minded artisans and farmers who were striving to get ahead—"laboring" men like Walter Brewster, Christopher Leffingwell, and William Manning.[30] These were the sorts of men that eventually became what self-made Boston printer, publisher, and editor Joseph T. Buckingham in 1830 called the "middling class"—the farmers, the mechanics, the manufacturers, the traders, who carry on, professionally the ordinary operations of buying, selling, and exchanging merchandize." These middling men were those who, in contrast to "the unproductive poor and the unprofitable rich," worked for a living and whose "unextinguishable desire for more" gave "birth to invention, and impart vigor to enterprise."[31]

Manning was one of these enterprising types. As Merrill and Wilentz concede, he certainly was no "injured little yeoman" uninvolved in a commercial economy.[32] He was much more than a small farmer in his little developing town of Billerica; he was as well an improver and a small-time entrepreneurial hustler. He ran a tavern off and on, erected a saltpeter works making gunpowder during the Revolutionary War, helped build a canal, bought and sold land, constantly borrowed money, and urged the printing of money by state-chartered banks, seeking (not very successfully, it seems) every which way to better his and his family's condition. By themselves Manning's commercial activities may not be much, but multiply them many thousandfold throughout the society and we have the makings of an expanding capitalist economy. Nevertheless, Merrill and Wilentz want to emphasize that these commercial activities "do not, in themselves, mark him . . . as a profit-maximizing individualist who believed in the universal justice of commercial markets." (There's that caricatured image of the profit-maximizer again.) Nor do all of Manning's commercial activities, write Merrill and Wilentz, "signal an attachment to capitalist enterprise." One could participate in all these commercial endeavors

"and still oppose capitalism (that is, a commercial economy dominated by moneyed men)."[33]

The difficulty seems to be with these "moneyed men." They
seem to inject a capitalist poison into an otherwise healthy commercial market economy. Who might they be? Merrill and Wilentz
apparently think Manning's few rich men who did not work for a
living were the moneyed men; they presumably supplied the capital for capitalist expansion. But these Federalist gentry, even if some
of them invested in businesses, represented much more the old
aristocratic order than they did the capitalist future. By themselves
they were never numerous or wealthy enough to finance the rise
of capitalism. As Bray Hammond pointed out forty years ago,
America in the late eighteenth century, unlike the Old World, had
a severe shortage of capital, the popular solution to which was
banks, lots of them.[34] In the early republic the capitalists that most
American entrepreneurs and borrowers, including Manning, actually relied upon were all those bankers in the proliferating state-
chartered banks. It was these banks' selling shares in bank stock
and issuing of hundreds of thousands of dollars of paper money
that supplied much of the capital that fueled the economy of the
early republic.[35]

Manning knew a great deal about modern paper money, and,
like many other Antifederalist or Republican entrepreneurs in these
years, he was a fervent defender of paper money and of state banks.
As Janet Riesman has said, it was Manning and others like him,
more than the Federalist "moneyed men," who saw that the primary source of America's wealth lay in its "internal productivity."
They came to appreciate that it was the energy and hard work of
America's laboring people, and not any great resources of specie,
that supported the credit of the bank notes.[36] Although Manning
was not "a profit-maximizing individualist who believed in the
universal justice of commercial markets," nevertheless he and his
hard-working Republican "laborers" were the main force behind
America's capitalist market revolution. For good or for ill, American capitalism was created by American democracy.[37]

In the end it was precisely because men like Manning were
not "profit-maximizing individualists who believed in the universal justice of commercial markets" that they were able to create a
viable capitalist society. Only in the past several years have we

come to appreciate fully what we have come to call a civil society—that network of social associations and organizations that stand between the individual and the state and that help to temper and civilize the stark crudities of a market society, indeed, that help to make a viable market society possible. One of the remarkable results of the American Revolution was the sudden emergence in the early republic of this sort of associational life or civil society. In the several decades following the Revolution hundreds and thousands of voluntary associations of all kinds sprang up, particularly in New England where presumably American capitalism was born.[38]

Probably the most important of these voluntary associations were the new evangelical religious organizations—Baptists, Methodists, New Divinity Congregationalists, and dozens of other new sects—that in three decades or so transformed the religious landscape of America. Most of the evangelicals in these new religious associations were not unworldly or anticapitalist. Quite the contrary: it was the involvement of people like Manning in these religious associations that helped to make possible the rise of capitalism. Evangelical religious passion worked to increase people's energy as it restrained their selfishness, got them on with their work as it disciplined their acquisitive urges. Even the New Divinity Calvinism to which Manning subscribed recognized, as William Britenbach and James D. German have pointed out, that "wicked self-interest was no threat to a moral economic order." The New Divinity theology "admitted a sphere within which self-interest was morally legitimate"; it gave people confidence that self-interested individuals nevertheless believed in absolute standards of right and wrong and thus could be trusted in market exchange and contract relationships.[39] Those who assume that a capitalist society requires mainly selfish individuals preoccupied with the bottom line do not understand the sources of America's capitalism in the early republic. It's time that we recognized who the capitalists in America really are: we have met the enemy and it is us.

NOTES

1. Stephen Innes, *Creating the Commonwealth: The Economic Culture of Puritan New England* (New York, 1995), 328.

2. *Ibid.*, 56.

3. Michael Merrill, "Putting 'Capitalism' in Its Place: A Review of Recent Literature," *William and Mary Quarterly*, 52 (Apr. 1995), 315–26; Merrill, "The Anticapitalist Origins of the United States," *Review: A Journal of the Fernand Braudel Center*, 13 (Fall 1990), 465–97.

4. For some reviews of the debate, see Robert E. Mutch, "Colonial America and the Debate about the Transition to Capitalism," *Theory and Society*, 9 (Nov. 1980), 847–63; Christopher Clark, "Economics and Culture: Opening Up the Rural History of the Early American Northeast," *American Quarterly*, 43 (June 1991), 279–301; Christopher Clark, ed., "The Transition to Capitalism in America: A Panel Discussion," *The History Teacher*, 27 (May 1994), 263–88; Gordon S. Wood, "Inventing American Capitalism," *New York Review of Books*, June 9, 1994, 44–49.

5. Winifred Barr Rothenberg, *From Market-Places to a Market Economy: The Transformation of Rural Massachusetts, 1750–1850* (Chicago, 1992).

6. *Ibid.*, ix.

7. Allan Kulikoff, *The Agrarian Origins of American Capitalism,* (Charlottesville, 1992), 8.

8. James A. Henretta, *The Origins of American Capitalism: Collected Essays* (Boston, 1991), 34.

9. Kulikoff, *Agrarian Origins of American Capitalism*, 19.

10. Henretta, *Origins of American Capitalism*, 92, 97; Christopher Clark, *The Roots of Rural Capitalism: Western Massachusetts, 1780–1860* (Ithaca, 1990), 84.

11. Never mind farmers—perhaps very few entrepreneurs or capitalists in the early republic were ever this kind of selfish, profit-maximizing individualist. We do not know this in fact because the moral economy historians have never actually analyzed the behavior of the "capitalists" and tested to see where and in what manner it differs from the behavior of the "non-capitalist" farmers. For the similarity of the commercial worlds of New England farmers and merchants, see Thomas Allen, "Commerce, Credit, and Community: The Transformation of Economic Relationships in Rhode Island, 1771–1850" (Ph.D. diss., Brown University, 1994).

12. Kulikoff, *Agrarian Origins of American Capitalism*, 2, 5, 4.

13. *Ibid.*, 4.

14. Innes, *Creating the Commonwealth*, 39.

15. Merrill, "Putting 'Capitalism' in Its Place," 322, 325, 323, 324.

16. *Ibid.*, 325, 322.

17. Bruce Laurie, "'Spavined Ministers, Lying Toothpullers, and Buggering Priests': Third-Partyism and the Search for Security in the Antebellum North," in Howard B. Rock, Paul A. Gilje, and Robert Asher, eds., *American Artisans: Crafting Social Identity, 1750–1850* (Baltimore, 1995), 100, 104; Gary J. Kornblith, "'Cementing the Mechanic Interest': Origins of the Providence Association of Mechanics and Manufacturers," *Journal of the Early Republic*, 8 (Winter 1988), 355–87, reprinted in Ralph D. Gray and Michael A. Morrison, eds., *New Perspectives on the Early Republic: Essays from the Journal of the Early Republic, 1981–1991* (Urbana, 1994), 103–35.

18. [John Adams], *Discourses on Davila: A Series of Papers on Political History* (1790; rep., New York, 1973), 91.

19. For general literature on artisans in this period, see notes 17 and 18 in Paul A. Gilje, "The Rise of Capitalism," in this volume.

20. As Stuart M. Blumin suggests, much of our confusion over what was happening socially in the late eighteenth century comes from our inability to appreciate the extent to which gentlemen were set off from all common people who had to work for a living, middling as well as poor. Blumin, *The Emergence of the Middle Class: Social Experience in the American City, 1760–1900* (Cambridge, 1989), 33–34.

21. Laurie, "'Spavined Ministers,'" in Rock, Gilje, and Asher, eds., *American Artisans*, 105. On Franklin's move from laboring artisan to gentlemen, see Gordon S. Wood, *The Radicalism of the American Revolution* (New York, 1992), 38, 85–86, 118–19. Even a distinguished painter like John Singleton Copley, because he worked with his hands, was regarded by his gentry patrons as just another artisan. For such gentry, Copley said bitterly in 1767, painting was "no more than any other useful trade, as they sometimes term it, like that of a Carpenter tailor or shoemaker." "Letters and Papers of John Singleton Copley and Henry Pelham, 1739–1776," Massachusetts Historical Society, *Collections*, 71 (1914), 661–66.

22. James P. Walsh, "'Mechanics and Citizens': The Connecticut Artisan Protest of 1792," *William and Mary Quarterly*, 42 (Jan. 1985), 66–89.

23. Even into the Jacksonian era some continued to argue that the "employer who superintends his own business, (still more if he works with his own hands) is a working man." Quoted in Laurie, "'Spavined Ministers,'" in Rock, Gilje, and Asher, eds., *American Antisans*, 104.

24. Kornblith, "Origins of the Providence Association," in Gray and Morrison, eds., *New Perspectives*, 132.

25. Michael Merrill and Sean Wilentz, eds., *The Key of Liberty: The Life and Democratic Writings of William Manning, "A Laborer," 1747–1814* (Cambridge, MA, 1993). For a superb study of the struggles of the Abbé Sieyes with these issues of work and leisure during the French Revolu-

tion, see William H. Sewell, Jr., *A Rhetoric of Bourgeois Revolution: The Abbé Sieyes and What is the Third Estate?* (Durham, 1994).

26. As Paul A. Gilje points out, following the Revolution "it became increasingly difficult to use *mechanic* as a slur word to denigrate men who earned their living by the sweat of their brow." Gilje, "Introduction. Identity and Independence: The American Artisan, 1750–1850," in Rock, Gilje, and Asher, eds., *American Artisans*, xiv.

27. See, for examples, William H. Sewell, *Work and Revolution in France: The Language of Labor and the Old Regime to 1848* (New York, 1980); Steven Laurence Kaplan and Cynthia J. Koeff, eds., *Work in France: Representations, Meaning, Organization, and Practice* (Ithaca, 1986); and Patrick Joyce, ed., *The Historical Meanings of Work* (New York, 1987).

28. Merrill and Wilentz, eds., *The Key of Liberty*, 127, 136, 137. Merrill and Wilentz have modernized Manning's texts, but in the process they have corrected all his phonetic spelling and thus removed some of the flavor of his writings. For an edition of "The Key of Liberty" that is closer to the original text, see Samuel Eliot Morison, ed., "William Manning's 'The Key of Libberty,'" *William and Mary Quarterly*, 13 (Apr. 1956), 202–54.

29. So confused have we become over the meaning of the bourgeoisie and other Marxist terms we use that some scholars have difficulty socially locating an aristocrat or landed gentleman like Madison. Because he cared a lot about property, he becomes "bourgeois" and thus presumably is to be placed in the same class as an upwardly mobile manufacturer like Christopher Leffingwell. For Madison as a bourgeois or liberal thinker, see Richard K. Matthews, *If Men Were Angels: James Madison and the Heartless Empire of Reason* (Lawrence, 1995).

30. This is the gist of Joyce Appleby's *Capitalism and a New Social Order: The Republican Vision of the 1790s* (New York, 1984). For further evidence, see the recent work of Kenneth Sokoloff on early patenting and productivity growth. Sokoloff, "Inventive Activity in Early Industrial America: Evidence from Patent Records, 1790–1846," *Journal of Economic History*, 48 (Dec. 1988), 813–50; Sokoloff and B. Zorina Khan, "The Democratization of Invention During Early Industrialization: Evidence from the United States, 1790–1846," *Journal of Economic History*, 50 (June 1990), 363–78; and Sokoloff, "Invention, Innovation, and Manufacturing Productivity Growth in the Antebellum Northeast," in Robert Gallman and John Joseph Wallis, eds., *American Economic Growth and Standards of Living Before the Civil War* (Chicago, 1992), 345–78.

31. Joseph T. Buckingham, *An Address* (1830), quoted in Gary J. Kornblith, "Becoming Joseph T. Buckingham: The Struggle for Artisanal Independence in Early-Nineteenth-Century Boston," in Rock, Gilje, and Asher, eds., *American Artisans*, 129.

32. Merrill and Wilentz, eds., *The Key of Liberty*, 31. Although Merrill and Wilentz deny (in the exaggerated imagery of the moral economy historians) that Manning was "an ambitious, individualistic petty capitalist who more than anything else simply wanted to get rich," Manning himself declared that all persons, "let their conditions in life be what they will," had "so strongly implanted in them a desire for self-support, self-defense, self love, self-conceit, and self-aggrandizement that it engrosses all their care and attention—so that they can see nothing beyond self." *Ibid.*, 205, 129.

33. *Ibid.*, 31–32. Historians unsympathetic to capitalism like Merrill and Wilentz tend to create straw images of a stark capitalist mentality, e.g., "a full and unproblematic devotion to the commercial market and its ethic," in order more easily to blow them away. *Ibid.*, 31.

34. Bray Hammond, *Banks and Politics in America, From the Revolution to the Civil War* (Princeton, 1957), 69.

35. J. Van Fernstermaker, *The Development of American Commercial Banking, 1782–1837* (Kent, OH, 1965); Naomi R. Lamoreaux, *Insider Lending: Banks, Personal Connections, and Economic Development in Industrial New England* (Cambridge, 1994). "Most of the funds that banks lent out (that is, most of the funds they used to support economic development)," says Lamoreaux, "came from sales of bank stock. Banks were particularly good at tapping the community's savings by getting people with accumulations as small as $100 to invest their resources in bank stock." Lamoreaux to author, July 24, 1995; and Lamoreaux, *Insider Lending*, 3, 19–22, 64–83.

36. Merrill and Wilentz, eds., *The Key of Liberty*, 103–09; Janet A. Riesman, "Money, Credit, and Federalist Political Economy," in Richard Beeman, Stephen Botein, and Edward C. Carter II, eds., *Beyond Confederation: Origins of the Constitution and American National Identity* (Chapel Hill, 1987), 156–61.

37. In the thirty years following the Revolution, for example, the once despised mechanics came to constitute one-half of the elected officials of the city of New York. Not that they were poor workingmen: their median wealth almost matched that of rich merchants. Nevertheless, the rise of common ordinary folk like these mechanics to positions of dominance in the early republic is usually what we mean by democratization; it is certainly what contemporaries meant by the rise of democracy. Edward Pessen, *Riches, Class, and Power Before the Civil War* (Lexington, MA, 1973), 297.

38. The best study of these voluntary associations in New England is Conrad Edick Wright, *The Transformation of Charity in Postrevolutionary New England* (Boston, 1992).

39. Merrill and Wilentz, eds., *The Key of Liberty*, 52–54; William

Britenbach, "Unregenerate Doings: Selflessness and Selfishness in New Divinity Theology," *American Quarterly*, 34 (Dec. 1982), 479–502; James D. German, "The Social Utility of Wicked Self–Love: Calvinism, Capitalism, and Public Policy in Revolutionary New England," *Journal of American History*, 82 (Dec. 1995), 965–98, (quotations at 998 and 983). For a sympathetic account of the role of religion in the development of the working class in the early republic, see Jama Lazerow, *Religion and the Working Class in Antebellum America* (Washington, DC, 1995).

CONTRIBUTORS

PAUL A. GILJE is Professor of History at the University of Oklahoma. He is author of *The Road to Mobocracy: Popular Disorder in New York City, 1763–1834* and *Rioting in America.*

JEANNE BOYDSTON is Associate Professor of History at the University of Wisconsin–Madison. She is author of *Home and Work: Housework, Wages, and the Ideology of Labor in the Early Republic* and co-editor of *The Limits of Sisterhood: The Beecher Sisters and Woman's Sphere.*

DOUGLAS R. EGERTON is Professor of History at Le Moyne College in Syracuse, New York. He is author of *Charles Fenton Mercer and the Trial of National Conservatism* and *Gabriel's Rebellion: The Virginia Slave Conspiracies of 1800 and 1802.*

CHRISTOPHER CLARK is Professor of History at the University of York, England. He is author of *The Roots of Rural Capitalism: Western Massachusetts, 1780–1860* and *The Communitarian Moment: The Radical Challenge of the Northampton Association.*

JONATHAN PRUDE is Associate Professor of History at Emory University. He is author of *The Coming of Industrial Order: Town and Factory Life in Massachusetts, 1810–1860* and co-editor of *The Country in the Age of Capitalist Transformation: Essays in the Social History of Rural America.*

RICHARD STOTT is Associate Professor of History Department at George Washington University. He is author of *Workers in the Metropolis: Class, Ethnicity, and Youth in Antebellum New York City,* and has edited William Otter's *History of My Own Times.*

CATHY D. MATSON is Associate Professor of History at the University of Delaware. She is author (with Peter S. Onuf) of *A Union of Interests: Political and Economic Thought in Revolutionary America.*

GORDON S. WOOD is Professor of History at Brown University. He is author of *The Creation of the American Republic, 1776–1787* and *The Radicalism of the American Revolution,* which won the Pulitzer Prize for history.

HISTORIOGRAPHIC INDEX

See also *General Index* on page 162.

GENERAL INDEX

See also *Historiographical Index* on page 157.